Footprints

FLORIDA WRITERS ASSOCIATION COLLECTION

VOLUME 13

Featuring Person of Renown Author

Marina Brown

ww.FloridaWriters.org

ISBN: 978-1-7375305-0-3

ACKNOWLEDGEMENTS

One-hundred-sixty-eight entries poured in from 122 FWA members, twenty-eight of whom submitted two entries. Posted without author names to a specially designed website accessible only by judges, submissions were read and scored. FWA is deeply indebted to them, and thanks each for their time, dedication, and expertise.

Each entry is presented as submitted, with only minor editing, if mistakes like missing quote marks, misspelled words, or forgotten periods happen to be caught during the audit stage. Entrants also took advantage of attending one of FWA's many Critique Groups near them, or using FWA's editing service, which offered special pricing. The quality of entries reflects the professionalism and growth of our members. Thank you, Bobbie Christmas, for managing that special editing service.

Thank you to Charles H. Cornell for the design of the cover for our 13th Collection volume: Florida Writers Association Collection, Volume 13, Footprints.

It is with heartfelt gratitude that FWA acknowledges Marina Brown's contribution to this publication. She had perhaps the hardest job of all – choosing only ten entries to be her favorites out of the sixty winning entries.

The eighth annual Youth Writers Collection Contest, created to provide our youth members an opportunity to become published authors, produced nine winners from thirty-five submissions, five of whom submitted two entries. FWA acknowledges and thanks our Youth Writers Groups, their Group Leaders and especially Mark H. Newhouse, Michael Farrell, and Paula Feuerstein for their efforts to accomplish this goal.

A special thanks to Leah Miller, Patti Walsh, Lamar Barnett, and Joan Levy for their assistance with proofreading and editing, and Arielle Haughee and Chrissy Jackson for successfully accomplishing the myriad of tasks needed to establish FWA as the new, ongoing, official publisher of our collection volumes.

Your Collection Contest Coordinators, 2021

Su Gerheim   JC Gatlin

CONTENTS

MARINA BROWN'S TOP TEN PICKS

FOOTPRINTS
FLORIDA WRITERS ASSOCIATION COLLECTION, VOL. 13

FOOTPRINTS
FLORIDA WRITERS ASSOCIATION COLLECTION, VOL. 13

FOOTPRINTS
FLORIDA WRITERS ASSOCIATION COLLECTION
YOUTH COLLECTION, VOL 8

INTRODUCTION
FOOTPRINTS
FLORIDA WRITERS ASSOCIATION COLLECTION, VOL 13

What delightful meanderings I have had! As recipient of the Florida Writer's Association's 2020 Published Book of the Year award for my novel, The Orphan of Pitigliano, I was gifted with another prize! I was asked to read and rank 60 short stories/poems written by a group of dazzling authors. The eight stories and two poems which I have chosen, are based on the theme, "Footprints." Many, many of the entries were remarkable for their originality and ingenious twists. The authors used the few words required for these submissions to introduce vivid characters with histories, to scatter fascinating details, and to bring the tension-filled arcs of their tales to often dramatic endings.

Though a selection process always has a bit of subjectivity, I applied some of the criteria used in large contests to help. I tried to choose entries that were not wholly predictable in their outcomes. I looked for stories that led me along a quickly grasped path to an ending that might have been unexpected, yet was compelling. Spelling, syntax and punctuation were evaluated as well.

The selections below I found to be variously, touching, tender, surprising, sad, thought-provoking, and just plain beautiful. But then, there were many which had those same characteristics which would have spilled over the ten choices I was allowed.

My congratulations to each of the sixty authors whom I read. Your work shows the artistry of the written word. You all are truly gifted writers. And to all others who toil in the gardens where metaphor, analogy, intent, and meaning grow, may you make wonderful bouquets of words, ones that will never wilt, but will change our lives with their fragrance.

Marina Brown, October 2021

May I Have This Dance?

Harry blew his nose, the conventional, outside way men like him had learned from their fathers was acceptable. He wiped the residual snot on the back of his hand and glanced in the right rearview mirror at his 300-lb frame. Not the best physique for a guy in his line of work. But he was agile enough for crawling under houses and into the attics of the homes he was hired to inspect. Damned good at it, in fact. Not so good at keeping a woman happy.

He pulled out his clipboard, and checked the houses he would look at today: an old two-story, then another unoccupied place out along Crosby Road, a dead-end track where share-croppers had once lived. Be better to tear a heap like that down, Harry thought. But if somebody wanted to assess how bad the roof leaked, he'd let them know for a hundred bucks. Besides, it'd be another chance to use the new toy, a prize he'd won at a builder's convention a couple of weeks before. Seemed like it'd be better for the cops than for home inspections, but what the hell, it made the day go by faster, and god knew, there was no reason to go on back to his own empty house.

Harry pulled what looked like a portable Geiger-counter with an attached TV screen from the bed of the Ford, along with a measuring tape, a screw driver, and a plastic bag to collect termite crap. It was all he needed to tell a buyer about the past life of a building and if it had been loved or not. That's how Harry felt sometimes. Alone in an abandoned house, he thought he could almost feel the boards reporting abuse, the plumbing, neglect. And he was finding that with his new-fangled tool, there was even more to learn.

Harry had been told that the first house was once occupied by a cantankerous spinster who'd refused to leave her Victorian refuge until carried out. Harry looked forward to admiring the old building methods with the thick beams of impenetrable wood, and real plaster that clung to the walls. He hoped the irascible old maid hadn't let things go. He imagined her sitting in a chair filled with mold spores, angrily poking a cat, and ignoring yellow water dripping from the tap. But he learned that things were different.

He began with his usual measurements, checking the welds around the lead pipes, looking for rat-eaten insulation on the wiring, then turned on "the instrument." He wasn't sure how the thing worked, but once up and going, images would appear on its screen. Harry could discern wear inside window frames, weakness in wall studs, invisible flaws that showed up with a blue-lit glow. Oily stains and botched repairs were revealed as if a smirking tattle-tale were leading Harry from room to room. Recently, he'd noticed something else. If he twisted a half-hidden dial on the bottom of the machine, he could see in even more detail. Now, fingerprints were evident, jelly smears turned red, footprints leading from room to room as if muddy feet tramped back and forth—all showed on the little screen in his hands.

The old maid's ancient carpet was worn and faded, but with the dial turned to High, Harry began to see outlines of shoes facing this way and that. In patterns, that when he actually put his own foot on one, and then another, Harry found himself turning, almost swaying, moving from print to print in what was surely a dance. Looking more carefully, he saw there were smaller feet facing opposite the larger ones— moving in synchrony. And they were everywhere—in the parlor, in the dining room, and even in the bedroom, where the patterns were tighter, less movement of feet, as if the old woman and her lover only swayed, maybe kissed, soon made love. Harry stood staring at the floor, feeling jealous at how the tips of their toes interlaced. He wished he could have watched them dance and repeat the pattern of their steps.

He headed out toward Crosby Road, to the last house of the day. The fields were flat here, rimmed by pine forests that were prized when the turpentine moguls held sway. Along the road, set back on even narrower dirt tracks, were lines of abandoned share-croppers' cabins, former slave quarters they'd paid with labor to buy. Harry had been inside a few—walls covered in yellowed newsprint, running water and electricity still innovations. Although the one he was to inspect was a little bigger than the others, he had no idea why anyone would want to buy it.

He got out in front of the little porch and gathered his equipment. Just for the heck of it, he turned on the instrument, because, when all was said and done, a fat, lonely country boy had little more to do than follow other people's footprints. Harry wondered if this is how it felt to be a peeping-tom, stealing glimpses of others' lives when you don't have one of your own. Then he shrugged that he only saw what they had discarded, and he didn't turn off his machine.

But before he could even step onto the porch, Harry saw them. In fact, it looked like a damned zoo. Quail tracks in the yard. The wiggle of a snake going under the steps. A possum had visited, a dozen squirrels, several raccoons by the size of their prints, a fox whose feet looked the size of a dog. Harry walked to the back of the cabin, where the machine revealed two new sets of prints—something that had four soft paws, and another with two human feet that had walked into the woods.

He stopped for a moment, looking around at the layers of green. Verdigris to olive, lime and chartreuse, the underbrush a black that turned blue in the light, and the cabin's greyed wood, striated with the reds of old pine sap as the grain had sagged into elegant undulations and swags. And suddenly Harry longed to stay here, in the quiet, in the beauty of lost things turned old without anyone being aware. He thought he'd like to do it too—just like this.

He put down his gear and the new toy that whispered the paths others had tread, and softly set out into the woods, wondering at the way ahead, yet somehow sure.

And he saw her there, just as he had expected, just as he had hoped—just as her narrow, arched footprints had predicted. A tall, black woman, alone with her pet, letting the pond's light sow diamonds in her hair. She turned to him, unafraid, with eyes that might have recently wept in good-bye to her house, but now silently acknowledged him.

And Harry, held out his hand, sure of his destination, at last sure of where he stood, and where he could rest, and said, "Excuse me, Miss. Would you care to dance? I can teach you where to put your feet."

—**Marina Brown**, author of the FAPA Gold-Medal-winning novels, Land Without Mirrors; Lisbeth; and the FWA published Historical Fiction Gold-Medal-winner, and 2020 published Book of the Year, The Orphan of Pitigliano.

1. Dirt Road Women

In our town, we have a relationship with roads.
We love them, in theory.
Dirt roads are not for the overly tidy; they are known
to meander into ruts on whim and obey the laws of water
by command.

We, who consider ourselves responsible for the accountable
presence of children and the (reasonable) absence of dirt,
dislike sand in the screens and tracked by heavily sneakered boys
through hallways all over town.
Dogs, while amenable in most other ways, cannot be
persuaded to wipe their feet.
Or take off their shoes.

Viewed from the main road, the stories remain untold
in paw-print-sprints and sneakers so fast--
only the weighty top impression is seen,
the heel having been carried by wings.
Come May, even dirt road women feel the pull of summer,
call a truce, and want to walk bare-toed in the sand.
Along the uneven blocks, reshaped by lakes and coves,
we tend each other's sunlit boys, all sweat and impossibly
big shoes.

My short road is quiet, so we walk in search, shading our eyes
and squint into the light that finds us, soft and warm. Soon, in June,
to be a punishment undeserved.

We are sleuths who don't have far to travel, and we follow
the clues we know: bike tires swerve in sugar sand, and pick up again.
Joy lives in the mismatched treads of uphill,
sifting silently to mystery, in sand without rain; granules of instants and
hours.

Footprints

Sun shines across the twin cove, just down and away from the road,
and tells me the time.

Over my shoulder, in a shutter-click for memory,
is our barefoot progress, soon to be indistinct as spirit.
We find them, as we know we will, by sound and rumor:
loud and gritty, shining and sweet, they are languorous as lizards,
and crazy as puppies let loose.

Deep ends of pools cannot contain them. Waterways and driveways;
too much freedom will come
too soon from our searching eyes, and proffered food. (our only secret
weapon)

Footsteps falling to sand; the price we pay while seconds tick.
Amid the lively tumult, dirt road women mourn
their tiny,
tricky
babies.

 **Juli Simon** is a professional
muralist who calls both
Windermere and Winter Garden
home. She believes words and
color are much the same; they are
fully themselves but can undergo
change with just a nudge and a lot
of patience.

2. Rosa's Angel

Rosa Mendoza hated Room 417. ICU? Big deal. Just meant more nurses, more often. She took a deep breath and held it a few seconds. The technique never helped much at the dentist's office and didn't help here. She wiped a sweaty palm on the sheet and reached for the water cup. Her hand shook.

She couldn't see behind her, but knew all sorts of equipment hung back there. Their beeps, clicks, ticks, and whirring reminded her of a funeral dirge at church. Happy thoughts.

Saturday night? So what? It meant she'd survived another day only to creep a day closer to dying. The doctors hadn't sugar-coated it. Without a transplant her weakening heart would soon die, which meant Rosa would also die.

She turned her head to look at her mother, felt the tug of the oxygen tube under her nose. Tears welled in Rosa's eyes. She tried to blink them away, but they ran down her cheeks anyway. "Mami, I don't want to die."

Their gaze met. Ana Mendoza's eyes teared. She responded in accented English. "Mija, don't think that. God is sending you an angel; I know it."

Rosa wiped her eyes and twisted the bedsheet. "I'm only sixteen. I want to graduate from high school, go to the prom with Gabriel, go to college, visit your homeland—"

"I don't want to hear any more about that, descarado." Ana shook her finger. "No more."

"He is not a low life. Gabriel and I connect, like we're part of each other."

"The connection he wants is in his bed."

"Mami, don't talk like that."

"That one will make you with baby and then forget who you are, like your father did to me. I came to America for you to have a good life, not that. You listen to me." She wagged her finger at Rosa. "Nothing good will ever come from him. Stay away."

Rosa didn't respond.

Her only joy the past eight months had been Gabriel Cortez. Their relationship started in school, where she struggled with algebra and he with literature. Each offset the other's weakness. They became study partners and joked about being a match made in heaven.

She thought about the conversation they had the night before. He'd sneaked into the hospital after her mother left.

"I hope you get your new heart, Rosa. I just hope it doesn't change you."

"No way. I'll still laugh at your silly jokes. We'll drink McDonald's milkshakes together and hang out. Nothing will change but our future."

"But, your heart is full of love and joy. What if your new one is empty?"

They held hands, fingers intertwined. Rosa's voice quivered. "You've made an enormous impression on my soul, like a giant footprint that will never go away. It's my soul that makes me who I am. Even with a new heart I will always share my soul with you."

"But you need a heart to live." He leaned over, moved her oxygen tube, and kissed her on the lips for the first time ever. He whispered, "I love you" and then scurried out.

She cried happy tears.

Rosa's remembrances were interrupted when Nurse Amanda entered. After checking the monitors and typing in her laptop computer, the night nurse slapped the lid closed with a flourish. She glanced from Ana to Rosa and back to her mother. "Dr. Hartman will be here shortly. Please don't leave." Her sneakers squeaked when she spun and walked out.

The two Mendoza women looked at one another, surprised that the doctor would be there on a Saturday night.

Thirty minutes later Dr. Hartman arrived in green surgical scrubs instead of his starched white shirt, blue or red tie, and starched lab coat. He grinned. "Well, young lady, our prayers have been answered. A heart has become available."

Rosa's stomach flip-flopped.

Her mother crossed herself and thanked Jesus.

The doctor rubbed his hands together. "Blood type, weight, size, age, and markers are perfect. It's like a match made in heaven."

Ana asked, "How soon will—?"

"The surgical team is arriving as we speak." He patted her arm and winked. "We'll see you upstairs shortly."

***

Rosa's head felt like a vice had been clamped around it. She tried to open her eyes, but only a sliver of light peeked through. Someone must have stuffed cotton in her mouth and run sandpaper down her throat. "Am I alive?" she croaked. She sensed more than saw her mother approach.

"Oh, mija, yes, you are. How do you feel?"

"I hurt." It even hurt to say the words.

7

"Doctor say that's normal. He say the operation go good. You will live long."

Rosa felt herself slide into a black hole.

She awoke several hours later and opened her eyes. After a couple of blinks Rosa saw her mother's bloodshot eyes.

"Mija, how are you?"

"Sad." The single word squeezed by parched lips.

Ana straightened. "You should be happy You have a new heart and will live long."

"I'm alive because someone else died. It's not fair."

"It is God's plan. Your job on earth is not done. He wants you to do more. Be happy you have a chance to do His wishes."

"But . . ." She drifted again into the void of sleep.

The next time she awoke, Rosa begged for water.

Nurse Amanda placed the tip of a straw into her mouth. "Just a few sips."

Rosa wanted more, but the vice had returned to squeeze her head. Hot coals shifted inside her chest.

Dr. Hartman appeared like a genie sprung from a bottle. "How are we doing this fine Monday morning?" He bent and pressed his stethoscope to her chest.

"I hurt, and I'm hungry."

He listened to various spots on her chest and both sides of her neck. "We'll order broth. Can't afford any bloating, nausea, or straining. We have a lot of healing to do."

Dr. Hartman shuffled to the foot of the bed and felt each ankle. He opened the laptop, stared at the screen for a moment, and then announced, "We have good sounds and circulation this morning. Our numbers are phenomenal. Tomorrow we start therapy, but today, we rest." He patted her arm and left as quickly as he arrived.

Rosa dozed on and off until evening. Upon awakening she asked, "Mami, have you heard from Gabriel?"

Ana's lower lip quivered, just like when she shared that Aunt Carolina had died.

Rosa's stomach clenched. She grabbed the bedrails. "What's wrong? Tell me."

Ana spoke with her head down. "Mija, Gabriel is dead from a car crash Saturday morning."

Rosa couldn't breathe. She shook the bedrails, tried to shout, but nothing came out.

Ana jumped up, wide-eyed, wringing her hands.

The beginnings of a thought wedged into Rosa's mind. Slowly she lay back, began to relax. A couple of deep breaths stilled her, and the thought took root. She smiled and reached for her mother's hand. "You were right, Mami."

"About what?"

A tear trickled down her cheek. "God's angel came and will be with me the rest of my life. His heart is my heart." Her voice quivered. "His name is Gabriel Angel Cortez."

Henry James Kaye was born and raised in Pittsburgh, and had successful careers in banking, entrepreneurship, technology, and now real estate. His passion—writing—produced multiple Collections stories, several published novels, and two RPLA winners. He married Nancy more than forty-five years ago, they have three children and one grandchild. He lives in Longwood, Florida.

3. Boots

When the gong rang for lights out, Jian was already lying on his bed, every nerve awake. This was it. His chance for freedom outside these four walls. For the possibility of a loving touch or a kind word.

He eased the rhubarb buns from the space between his bed and the wall. It hadn't been easy to save so many buns. Dessert on his meal tray was scarcer than a belly rumble at a banquet. The buns were halfway to his mouth when he froze. Footprints. The floor guard was early.

Throwing himself to the floor, he peered through the crack under the heavy wooden door. The cool stone scraped against his cheek as he inched forward.

A pair of dusty leather boots hesitated outside the door. Jian raised an eyebrow. Hot and dry again today.

The world had moved on for the past five years while Jian passed the time in his musty room by counting the hairs sprouting from his chin (nine hairs today). For a third of his life, he hadn't breathed the scent of warm sunshine or tilted up his face to catch the first raindrops from a dark, murmurous sky. Footprints, the floor guard, was his only window to the changing life outside his room.

On hot, dry days, dust clung to the guard's boots, cracked leather curling back from the worn soles. These boots left dusty footprints on the cobbled stone floor.

On cool, rainy days, the sound of Footprints's feet squelching around his boots reached Jian's ears long before the guard did. Wet footprints dried slowly on the ground after Footprints left.

On cold, snowy days, the guard's wool-clad feet made little sound. The boots left small mounds of snow in the shape of footprints outside Jian's door. Now that his hands were larger, Jian could usually brush a finger against the snow before it melted. The shock of its icy touch was enough to send him into shivers for hours.

For this day, the day of his escape and the first day of his new life, dry weather gave him the best chance of survival. On rainy or snowy days, the path down the mountain was a ticket to broken bones and frozen toes. Now was his chance.

Footprints paused outside Jian's door, stooped, and pushed a small metal plate through the space between door and ground.

Jian paused only to register the day's meal, white rice with mustard-green cabbage, before leaping to his feet and sliding into the bed. His heart thrummed against his chest. Footprints knocked three times on the door.

Silence crept from the corners of the room and settled against Jian's ears. He was supposed to knock against his bed three times to let the guard know he was in the room. He'd done so every day for the last five years. Footprints never responded. Jian had never heard his voice or seen his face. He didn't even know the guard's real name.

Jian would see the guard's face that day.

Instead of speaking, Jian took a deep breath and smeared rhubarb under his nose and down the front of his tunic.

Footprints knocked again. Jian waited two heartbeats and then called out in a weak voice, "There's something wrong with me, sir."

The lock clicked. With a screech, the door swung into the room, and Footprints stood silhouetted in the doorway. A shaft of light fell across Jian's face. He closed his eyes as his head fell back on the bed.

The guard grunted, and there was a note of hesitancy in the sound of his feet as he stepped into the room. After a beat, he scooped Jian into his arms. Jian let his arms and legs flop as Footprints dashed out of the room. The guard's boots scraped against the ground as he turned a corner. A few more seconds, and they would be outside, running along the path between the prison and the infirmary.

Warm, fresh air, perfumed with the lush smell of growth and life, rushed into Jian's nose. He couldn't help drawing its flavor deep into his lungs. It was the scent of freedom, of a summer afternoon stretched out on grass, leaves tickling his cheek. So close.

With a jolt, Footprints stopped. Jian's eyes popped open. They widened, and he choked on dust as he inhaled sharply.

Footprints was a woman.

The guard dropped him, and he landed on the stone floor like an overripe melon. His attention fell on her boots, streaked with dirt and a hands-width away from kicking his face. He rolled over and spotted the door to the outside. It was halfway ajar, waiting for him.

Before he could scramble toward it, the door slammed shut. The fresh air disappeared, replaced with the stagnant underground air of the prison. Another guard moved from behind the door and grabbed his arm. Jian turned to Footprints.

The woman stared at him, eyes white in her brown face. "He's so young," she said to the other guard, her voice coming out in a gasp. The other guard shrugged and led Jian back to his room.

Three more steps, and he would have escaped.

Footprints was his guard for six more days before she was replaced. In those six days, she slipped more rhubarb buns, sweet egg tarts, and candied fruits under his door than he'd eaten in his entire life. He tasted more love in those days than in all the days up to his escape attempt. She never knocked on his door. Instead, she knelt next to the opening underneath and whispered into the dark, "Little boy, I am here for you."

But she wasn't. The new guard wore clean boots every time they walked past his room. Jian's connection to the outside world was gone, severed from his life as cleanly as Footprints had been. All that was left were the footprints pressed into his heart.

Jessie Erwin is a registered dietitian who finds food often sneaks into her writing. When she's not offering nutrition advice or burning her latest batch of fried rice, Jessie writes fiction, raises three kids, and tackles her mission of tasting every kind of chocolate in the world.

4. WhipLash

If luck were his aftershave, he'd smell like a restaurant dumpster. He didn't mean for it to happen, but there lay the famous novelist Loralia Ropert – on the floor, dead.

"Damn it." He smacked his forehead with the heel of his palm pacing up and back. He formed a mental checklist of how to erase his presence as her current lover. First, remove any recent photos from her cell phone. Next, check her house for any items he may have left here. He wouldn't need to remove all his fingerprints since it was common knowledge that he'd visited her several months ago, just the incriminating ones.

How long had it been since they'd begun their affair? Tears welled; he shook his head. No time for remorse. He decided to stage this disaster to look like a break-in gone fatal. He'd go out through the French doors, down the back steps to the beach and around to the front door to perform a real break-in. He bounded out the doors before his emotions could take over.

Before stepping up to the front window, he paused and kicked wet sand off the bottoms of his worn deck shoes. Footprints were often the key to solving crimes, and he didn't want to leave his. Getting caught would end his career and his marriage.

Grabbing gloves, he shifted to burglar mode, peering in the window. It was open! The screen eased out; he eased in with a jump. An hour later he exited out the window, tossing the screen in the bushes and drove away in his 1979 two-tone Dodge Aspen, confident he'd erased his intimate connection.

***

The population of Hapalie Island shrank to a teaspoon every summer. Loralia wrote all her novels from her secluded beach house, sanctioning the town to advertise its celebrity status and raising rental rates. Rumors circulated that she engineered personal adventures to write about but it was a known fact that she visited the post office daily. When Loralia didn't pick up her fan mail, the postmaster alerted the police.

Whip and Lash Harnen were the county's detectives and twin brothers. They appeared posthaste on the scene. An attractive luminary like Ms. Ropert was held in the highest esteem, even higher than the winner of the annual Oyster-Eating Contest.

WhipLash, as the pair were known around town, found her body splayed on the kitchen floor, with a dent in her forehead. Near her body lay a chef's knife, a candlestick, rope, a wrench, and blood splatters. Each detective snapped on gloves and performed his own assessment of the premises.

Afterward they knelt by Loralia's body and shared their findings. Whip said, "My initial impression tells me she slipped or was pushed, hitting her head on this corner here." He pointed to the counter edge, then shifted her head with the end of his pen to reveal a bloody gash on the back of her head. "She surprised an intruder and he hit her when she tried to defend herself with any one of these random objects."

Lash interrupted. "What indicates there was an intruder?"

Whip explained his theory. "Well, the knife is out of its holder. There doesn't appear to be anything she was cutting. Someone is clearly trying to send us a message by leaving this tableau. All we need is a lead pipe and revolver and we'd have a game of Clue."

"We played that as kids." Lash grinned, "Hey, that'd be something fun you, me and the wives to play one night."

"How about we stay focused on this crime scene?"

Lash cleared his throat and looked at his notes. "The drawers of that huge jewelry box in the master bedroom were open. I spotted a pregnancy test on the bathroom counter which indicates a male or male persons in her life, who may or may not be involved. Point of entry could have been the unlocked window." Lash snapped his fingers, his face animated, "I got it. What if that scum ex-husband of Loralia's came back into her life? She tells him she's knocked-up and they have a fight because he doesn't want to leave his new wife. They only live in the next town over." Lash pantomimes dropping a mic.

"Don't you think that's a little farfetched? Why would he rekindle with Loralia if he has a bride?" Whip checked his notes. "Did you happen to notice the footprint on the tile inside the front window?"

Lash paled. "You mean the dirt?"

"It's sand in the distinct pattern of a distinct deck shoe called Floafers."

Whip showed Lash the photo on his phone. "See, you can make out part of their signature stamp FLO..ERS. I wouldn't have caught it if I didn't just see them online."

"One shoeprint. So, we're looking for a one-legged guy?"

Whip shook his head. "We came here a few months ago to file Loralia's complaint about her ex-husband, remember? Maybe you're right about him."

Lash beamed like he'd just solved world hunger. "Maybe he was looking for a ring he wanted back or something."

Whip shrugged. "I'll track him down."

***

Whip heard Lash's car engine chug to the dock and he watched him change shoes inside his car. He yelled to Lash, "How's your Asss-pen?"

Lash walked toward a laughing Whip. "Don't you ever get tired of asking that?"

"Never."

They loaded their boat, The Snidely, for a day of fishing. Whip pushed the boat into the water, and something caught his eye. He aimed his phone toward the thick mud and snapped a photo, then sprang onto the skiff.

They put their lines in the water. Hours of trawling passed. Whip broke the quiet, "Check out this photo."

"Looks like crime scene footprint." Lash said. "Does it match the ex's?"

"Nope. Besides, the ex has an alibi. This photo's from earlier today."

Lash slowly turned his foot over to see the bottom of his shoes. "Son of a bitch. I only wear these when I'm around water.

Whip stared at Lash. "I got the clue. Why don't you tell me what happened, Lash? Did Loralia want more than an affair?"

Lash hung his head.

Whip pressed on. "You thought she was pregnant, so you decided to silence her?"

Lash jerked his head up. "Hell no. I knew that test was a prop. Coroner said she wasn't pregnant. She wanted me to open a bottle of wine. Told me we were drinking to a plot twist for her book. I yanked the cork out so fast, my elbow smashed into her forehead. She fell back against that corner ... I swear it was an accident."

Whip's hand squeezed his brother's shoulder. "Don't sweat it, Bro. I was seeing her too. Evidence points to both of us."

"What ...?"

Whip removed his own deck shoe holding it bottom side up. FLOAFERS, like Lash's, only newer.

15

Lash's wide eyes looked at his brother exploding with gratitude. His luck had changed.

***

The WhipLash boys blithely presumed Loralia's case would become cold—until they each received a copy of Loralia's final manuscript in the mail—about twin detectives. Her story treaded too close to their Hapalie home.

Fern Goodman is an RPLA award-winning author, a poet, and humorist, with her latest memoir Knee(d) to Know on Amazon. Her short stories appear in many FWA's Collections, various other anthologies, and magazines.

"Creativity is my lifeline, without laughter there is no soul. I'm serious about that."-FG

5. A Path Without Footprints

The '67 Camaro blasted through the winter dawn. As the car neared the last hill, Donna mashed the gas pedal to feed the V-8 engine. With a defiant roar, the beast charged up the steep incline. The icy road tried—and failed—to tame the aggression, the slick slope causing only the slightest shimmy as the Camaro left tire prints on virgin snow.

Donna couldn't keep a grin off her face. She patted the dashboard and basked in the glory of conquest. A two-story apartment building appeared through ice-covered oaks. She eased off the accelerator and the muscle car coasted contemptuously into an empty parking spot, next to a cowardly Prius. Donna honked the horn, a braying beckon to her son, Brian. She slugged her own fuel, a gulp of Dunkin' coffee sweetened with cream and three sugar packets. Although only lukewarm, it tasted like victory champagne.

The apartment's front door slammed closed, and snow cascaded off an overhang onto a handsome teen who brushed frozen flakes from his brown hair. Brian had the same rangy build as his father, who thankfully did not make an appearance. The divorce was still raw, the scab of a failed marriage torn off whenever they squabbled about how to raise their son.

From Brian's scowl, Donna expected a reproach for driving the Camaro in the season's worst weather. Brian shared that trait with his father—questioning behavior through the lens of logic. He didn't appreciate her emotional need for speed. What was life without simple pleasures? If only she could make him understand.

The passenger door groaned open. Brian shoved a trumpet case into the backseat and dropped his backpack onto the floorboard. "Ugh. It's freezing." He turned toward her and frowned. "No heat?"

The car backed out of its parking spot. She shrugged. "Sorry. It's on the fritz." She pointed to the tumbler on the console between the seats. "I bought you hot chocolate to make up for it. Put it in the Yeti to keep it warm."

"You know chocolate makes me break out."

"Yeah, well, I'll make sure your father buys more Neutrogena. Live a little."

Brian sighed, slipped off his gloves, and wrapped his fingers around the mug. Steam rose out of the opened lid, and the sugary aroma of cocoa filled the car. He took a small sip. "Where's the Subaru?"

Donna shrugged again. "Gave it the day off."

Brian took another sip and stared out into the blizzard. "Seriously? It's days like this that beg for four-wheel drive. I don't understand why you insist on driving this thing."

The engine snarled, and the vintage vehicle surged forward. Donna sipped more coffee, her knees holding the steering wheel in line. "I love this old girl. She's not a thing."

Brian crossed his arms. "This dinosaur gets less than six miles to the gallon. Haven't you heard about reducing your carbon footprint, Mom?"

"That's why I have a Subaru and drive the Camaro once a week." She shifted into a higher gear. "This was your grandfather's car and driving it reminds me of him. What good is saving the planet if there's no joy left in it?"

Brian stared out the passenger window. His brow furrowed. A snowplow heaved slush onto the road's shoulder. He took another sip from the tumbler. "I miss Grandpa, too. Thanks for the hot chocolate."

Donna let out a long breath. "No problem, kiddo. You set for school?"

"I guess."

"Geometry test today, right?"

"Yeah. And before you ask, I studied."

Donna let the comment go—of course he'd studied for it. His father wouldn't let that slide. "And then band after school?" The car coasted down the hill to the traffic light. "Did you have time to practice?"

"Not really."

Donna tapped the steering wheel with her fingers. The signal turned green, and the Camaro charged, leaving a lumbering SUV behind. She wanted Brian to have more balance in his life. Music. Art. Athletics. "Hmm."

"Don't start."

"What?"

"You disapprove."

"You don't enjoy playing?"

"I'm not any good at it."

The road curved around another hill, twisting its way toward the river. Donna bit her lip. "You didn't answer my question."

Brian kicked his backpack. "What does it matter? If I can't make first chair, why should I bother?"

"That's your father talking."

Brian slouched in his seat. "Ugh."

"Hear me out." She shifted the engine into a higher gear. "Sometimes you need to do things because you enjoy them. It doesn't matter whether you're good at it. Guilty pleasures relieve stress."

Brian flipped the tumbler lid open. Then closed. Then open again. "Dad thinks I should quit. He says it would leave more time to study for the SAT."

Donna clenched her teeth. She'd given Brian her old trumpet, hoping he'd enjoy music. They crested a hill, and a three-story brick high school came into view through the swirling snow. "Screw him."

"Mom!"

"Oh, please. You say worse to your friends on the phone."

Brian blinked, then smirked. "So you think it's okay—"

"To have a hobby? Goof off once in a while? Yeah. Blaze your own trail. Sometimes the best path is the one without footprints."

The car rumbled and went quiet as it neared the drop-off point in front of the school, like a lioness approaching a watering hole. Plumes streamed from a line of tailpipes. Some kids trudged along sidewalks with their heads tucked to avoid the wind. Others took shortcuts to the front door and plowed through shin-deep snow.

Brian finished his drink. "You think Grandpa would have liked to hear me play?"

The Camaro stalked forward. "Are you kidding? He would have recorded every halftime show and concert. And then he'd force his poker buddies to watch them in the senior home."

Brian smiled. "You mentioned a path without footprints. Were you serious?"

"Yeah."

"I know you gave me the horn you played in college. What if I want to switch instruments? Play a mellophone?"

Donna's eyebrows rose. "Why the mellophone?"

"I like the way it sounds. Different key. Deeper tone. Richer. Dr. Clark wants volunteers. More balance in the band. He's got a couple school-owned horns he can lend out."

The car came to rest under the portico of the school's front entrance. Donna relaxed in her seat. "Sounds perfect. I'll talk to your father."

Brian laughed. He opened the passenger door, stepped out, and retrieved his trumpet case and backpack. He stuck his head back in the car. "Thanks, Mom. Are you picking me up after band practice?"

"I'll be here. 4:30, right?"

"Yeah." He paused. "It's okay if you pick me up in the Camaro."

"What about my carbon footprint?"

Brian shrugged. "I guess it's okay to live a little." He closed the passenger door and waved goodbye.

Donna waved back. She was still smiling when the Camaro growled and raced out of the parking lot, leaving a new set of wild tire prints in its wake.

David M. Pearce was traumatized as a child by Willy Wonka & the Chocolate Factory and fears he will one day blow up into a blueberry, only to be rolled away by Oompa Loompas. He writes questionable stories using crayons—the fat ones.

6. Beyond the Closed Door

Trevor sprang awake to the clatter of jingle bells out in the hallway. He clenched Beary, his favorite stuffed animal, as a single thought filled his mind: Santa Claus.

His bare feet hit his bedroom floor. He dropped Beary, snatched the Batman flashlight he kept on his dresser, and dashed for his door. Hinges creaked and a door handle clicked. Trevor hesitated, fearing Santa might have heard him.

Heavy footsteps on hardwood followed by a metal screech let Trevor know he was probably detected.

Biting the side of his lip, he considered returning to bed. But his curiosity wouldn't let him. Trevor pushed open his door and tiptoed down the hallway toward the living room.

He stopped and clicked on his flashlight. Mommy's baking flour and a half-dozen tiny jingle bells littered the floor between the unlit Christmas tree and the hallway. He'd set this trap for Santa, giving the eight-year-old concrete proof of the jolly man's existence. Trevor squeaked at the sight of jingle bells' positions near the wall, kicked away from where he'd carefully placed them hours before.

He swung the beam of light up the hallway and noticed flour-laden footprints leading toward the closet that Trevor had been forbidden to enter during Christmas. Excited, he scurried for the closet and reached for the handle.

He balked.

Thoughts of his fellow second graders' teasing laughter a couple weeks ago consumed his mind. They pointed at him and told everyone how stupid he was that he still believed in Santa. He ran home that day crying. He buried his head in his pillow and thought about the closet. As much as he didn't want to admit it, the other kids' painful, "There's no Santa," made sense. If Mommy and Daddy bought the presents, they would have hidden them in the closet. He crept to the closet that day while Mommy cooked dinner and awaited Daddy's arrival from work. He couldn't open it then. Behind that door marked the end of something within him—something fragile and precious. Opening the closet door and seeing the presents meant he could never believe in Santa again, never believe in his magic, and never be that excited little boy at Christmas.

Now, he felt the same fear. There could be a Santa behind that door. Or, there still could be presents. The flour footsteps next to Trevor's bare feet could have just been Daddy's. He might have gotten up to pee. Or worse, stepped out in the night to retrieve the presents Trevor wasn't supposed to know about, in which case the closet would be empty, as empty as the magic he'd wished existed.

Slowly, Trevor backed away from the closet. He stared for a long, thoughtful moment, his insides pulling him in two directions.

Working up the courage, he opened his mouth rather than the door. "Santa?" he whispered. And then, slightly louder, "Santa Claus?"

No answer.

He waited longer.

Still no answer.

This didn't mean Santa wasn't in there. He could have been hiding, waiting for Trevor to leave. But he knew... he knew the closet was empty. No Santa. No magic.

His chin quivered as he fought the urge to cry. "It's okay, Santa." A tear trickled down his cheek. "I won't tell." He wiped his nose. "I know you're in there. But I won't tell."

He spun and crept back to his bedroom, smudging the flour footsteps beneath his bare feet. In his room, he dropped his flashlight onto his dresser, collapsed into bed, and buried his head into his pillow.

***

Donny waited a good few minutes before he opened the closet door, a switchblade still in his grip. Surveying the darkened hallway, the black-jacketed teenager stepped forward, careful this time not to kick the stupid jingle bells that had lined the floor.

Glancing down the hallway, he spotted the lopsided purse sitting on a narrow table. He rummaged the purse and found cash and jewelry and loaded his small fanny pack. Donny knew better than to bring anything bigger than his trusty fanny pack when robbing these upper middle-class houses. Just enough to get by without alarming these rich dweebs.

A sigh from the bedroom at the end of the hall alerted him. He froze.

He remained a statue, listening.

Nothing for long moment, then another sigh¬—it must have been that kid who was talking to him through the closet door. The noise came from the cracked open door further down the hall. Donny crept forward for the door. He peered in. A skinny kid in reindeer pajamas lay face-down, one leg dangling off one side. He moved to leave, when the kid mumbled, "No… no, there is a Santa. There is…"

The innocence of the boy's words awakened something deep and warm within Donny. Something he hadn't considered since he'd been a scrawny punk himself a decade back. The mocking laughter of friends telling him there was no Santa ignited a flame within. His boyhood tears gave way to fists, which gave his classmate a bloodied lip and Donny another trip to the principal's office.

Instincts told him to leave. He'd already been there too long and there were at least another few houses he planned on hitting before sunrise. Yet, the pull to the boy felt stronger.

He took a heavy breath and stepped into the room.

***

"Good morning, sweetie," Mommy said as she shook Trevor awake.

The boy arched his back and struggled to open his eyes. "Mommy?"

"It's Christmas morning."

Trevor's eyes popped open. He sat up. "Did Santa come?" But the moment the words left him, he recalled last night—his call to the closet with no response, his sad walk back to bed.

"Of course. C'mon." She stood and stepped for the door. She stopped, looking down. "How'd flour get in your room?"

Trevor remained silent.

Mommy frowned at the messy floor, then left the room.

Trevor wanted to race out to the Christmas tree, but sadness weighing inside held him back. Even if there were presents, he knew they probably weren't from Santa.

He stood next to his bed and glanced at his dresser where his Batman flashlight lay on its side. He moved for the door, but something next to the flashlight caught his eye—a folded piece of paper beneath a pencil.

He picked up the paper, opened it, and read. His heart leapt with joy. He wanted to share the letter with everyone, but he knew nobody, not even his parents, would have understood. He tucked the letter into his drawer, and throughout that day and every Christmas day for years to come, he recited every word in his heart:

Hey, Kid.

Thanks for not opening the closet door. That would have spoiled the magic.

Your pal, Santa.

John Hope is an award-winning short story, speculative fiction, historical, and young adult fiction writer. His work appears in various anthologies, in print, audiobooks, and adapted into plays. Mr. Hope, a native Floridian, loves to travel with his wife, Jaime, and two kids and enjoys running. Read more at www.johnhopewriting.com.

7. Kara Michaels

Kara Michaels ditched her mountain bike in the trees lining the edge of Cranberry Estates, one of several new housing projects taking root in Manatee County. The thirty-pound rucksack strapped to her back made the trip more difficult than usual.

She scanned the site. The silhouettes of several partially built structures jutted up from the flat plain. A half-moon added just enough light to the starry midnight sky that Kara didn't need a flashlight. She checked her perimeter continually as she shuffled toward the housing development. Although she'd dressed in black, she knew her outfit provided only limited stealth.

Kara located the address where they'd recently extended the sidewalk. Her hiking boots crushed gravel until she reached the excavations into which construction crews recently poured fresh cement. She walked along the edge of a series of squares, then got into position facing the two-story home whose construction had nearly finished.

She stepped over the wooden threshold and placed her left foot firmly in the cement about six inches from the edge. Her foot sank, but just a little. She shifted her weight forward while carefully maintaining her balance and placed her right foot next to her left.

As her torso swayed from side to side, her hiking boots sank ever so slightly into the hardening mixture. Her feet didn't sink as easily as before.

When Kara first started leaving her footprints throughout the job sites strewn about Manatee County, she had little trouble leaving her mark, but it looked like the contractors were catching on to her. They'd poured the cement mix early in the morning.

Still, it took twenty-four hours for the mixture to harden, then a month beyond that for it to fully set. Her feet sunk an acceptable quarter-inch, thanks to the extra thirty pounds on her back.

Once Kara felt confident she'd gone as deep as she could go, she stepped back to examine her handiwork. Two perfect footprints faced the two-story home. The letter 'K' adorned the middle of the left footprint, in the exact spot where she'd carved the rubber out of the sole of her hiking boot. In a similar fashion, the letter 'M' proudly graced the center of the right footprint.

Success. Kara pumped her fist. Then she hustled off towards her bicycle. Once there, she dumped the sand in her backpack and rode her bike back home.

***

The following morning, Florida-licensed building contractor Dave Parker drove his pickup to the Cranberry Estates work site. Several workers milled around the cement square in front of the two-story house. He stepped out of his truck and joined them.

"Don't tell me she struck again," he said.

"We won't tell you if you don't want us to, but see for yourself."

Another worker scratched his head. "How many is that?"

Dave sighed. "Over the past three years, officially, that's footprint set number twenty-seven."

"Well," said another man, "at least she's consistent."

A new hire asked, "Do we fix these things or leave them be?"

"It's the same old story." The older worker pointed. "If we grind it down and patch it, it affects the consistency of the cement and it'll likely crack. We can wait till it sets some more, then pound this section down to rubble and replace it, but that'll take time and money."

"At least a thousand bucks." Dave rubbed his thumb and index finger together. "Nope, it's not worth the effort. Leave it. If the owner complains, we'll deal with that later. So far, nobody's raised a stink."

"Why don't you try to catch this girl?"

"Because the additional security costs would be exorbitant. We have her on video. She's a blond-haired youngster who dresses in black and always wears a face mask. Aside from my speculation that she's intensely focused on making a name for herself, that's all we know."

"In other words," the new guy said, "it ain't worth the effort to fix it."

"Heck, I'm losing more money standing out here talking to all of you." Dave clapped his hands. "What do you say we all get back to work?"

***

Four months later, Ivan Tronka moved into his brand new, two-story home. He decided to go for a walk after a light rain shower dusted his lawn and driveway. When he turned onto the front sidewalk, he noticed two puddles shaped like footprints. The standing water reflected the sky but for two islands the shape of a 'K' and an 'M.'

He stomped back into his home and got on the line with the contractor. "It's still under warranty, and I want it fixed," Ivan barked at Dave.

At the cost of $1218, Dave hired a crew to remove the vandalized cement slab and place a fresh one in its place.

Kara Michaels succeeded in placing her footprints in front of thirty-three of the five-thousand-odd homes Dave built in Manatee County before she left Florida to chase her dreams. Of those thirty-three homes, Ivan Tronka was the only owner who complained.

***

Fifteen years later, Dave Parker and his wife accepted an all-expenses-paid trip to Los Angeles. It was the first time he'd ever flown first class. He was going to attend a ceremony honoring an old friend.

Though thousands of onlookers crowded Hollywood Boulevard, his hostess made a special point to have her aide guide Dave and his wife to front-row seats.

The pride of Manatee County, world-renowned singer-songwriter and recording artist Kara Michaels was about to receive her star ceremony at the Hollywood Walk of Fame.

"I'm glad you could make it," she told him.

Dave watched proudly as Kara, dressed in a black blouse, black slacks, and her favorite hiking boots, placed her footprints on the cement square. Kneeling, she impressed her handprints and drew her signature with a stick.

***

The value of Manatee County's thirty-two official "Kara homes" skyrocketed, easily garnering an additional $100,000 or more at sale. Owners who grew tired of the constant flow of pilgrims coming to Manatee County to "Cruise the K-M's" always felt better when bidding wars inflated the values of their homes.

Taking advantage of the strong housing market, Ivan Tronka eventually listed his house. His real estate agent insisted he'd make a fair profit on the sale.

"Too bad you didn't luck into owning one of those Kara homes," the agent told him. "Then I'd be able to list your property for an extra hundred grand."

Ivan sighed. "Yeah. Too bad."

Bart Huitema is the father of two teenage kids who have grown too old and sophisticated for bedtime stories. He now gets his story-telling fix by writing down his tales and sharing them with others.

8. Under-Standing

I didn't have to lash out at him with such cruelty.
The sand is soft and warm yet unstable,
awkward to walk on.
        No, he is not perfect.
        Some people say he deserved my tongue lashing.
With reverence, I stand in the vast, forgiving ocean.
I offer ho'oponopono prayer for exoneration.

"I'm sorry."
Cool water envelops my toes.
Nerve endings tingle in the salt water.
        I used to take pride in the clever way I could insult others.
        Now, I realize I am no better than a bully.

"Please forgive me."
Sea foam licks at my ankles.
        Does hurting him fix my hurting?
        It only feeds anger.
        Anger is a response to pain.

"I love you."
Waves ascend and collapse
as if dancing in an expression of requited love.
        No, the pain stops here with me.
        I will not perpetuate heartache any further.
        It is time for understanding.
        It is time for forgiveness.

"Thank you."
Under my feet, the sand releases to the ocean.
        The relationship cannot be fixed.
        I can only heal my own heart.
My footprints are erased by the waves
like my old way of being.

Who I am to judge?
It is what it is.

There is balance in movement,
one foot in front of the other.
    My prayer of forgiveness is for me.
    I deserve to be happy.
    We both do.
White caps of peace cleanse me.
    I cut the cords with grace.
    I will manage without him.
My spirit soars with seagulls.

Sonja Jean Craig is an award winning poet and the Secretary of Florida State Poets Association. Her guidance cards, A Love Affaire With Life, includes her poetry and photographs. She is published in several anthologies including Isolation Challenge, FSPA's Cadence, Fresh Fish and Poetic Visions.

9. Taking a Powder

Once a luxurious estate, Rest Haven now served as a private mental health facility.

The nurse smiled. "I'm sure you'll have a pleasant stay."

Ryan, in his immaculate Armani suit, nodded to the nurse.

"Don't be long. She needs her rest." The nurse left them.

Ryan turned to his wife. "You'll be fine in no time, Madeline."

She glared at him from the bed.

"Rest."

Madeline crumpled and crushed a fist full of the sheet covering her legs.

"I've two weeks off to organize the house, get the children adjusted." He cleared his throat. "Should be enough time for you to…recuperate."

Ryan edged closer to the door. "I'll stop back soon. We'll discuss the other matter then." He slithered out.

Madeline stood, stretched, and gazed at the woman sleeping in the other bed. The woman opened her eyes and studied Madeline with a clenched half-smile.

Madeline squared her shoulders. "I'm not crazy."

"Why are you here?" the woman asked.

A flush creeped across Madeline's face. "A well-deserved rest."

"People don't come here to rest."

Madeline took a step back. "I show my emotions, raise my voice once in sixteen years. That doesn't make me a mental case."

"Really?"

"See how long you'd last with my kids. Jamie's two, the twins are four and my daughter, Vickie, is a self-obsessed teenager."

"Anything else?"

Madeline frowned. "I cooked, cleaned, and ironed for sixteen years then Ryan comes home, late as usual and says, 'I'm in love with Jennifer. I want a divorce.'"

"What did you do?"

"I picked up Ryan's dinner – spaghetti and meatballs and chucked it. He ducked, it hit the wall, noodles clung to my wallpaper, red sauce splattered and meatballs rolled." Her eyes brightened. "That was the first time I didn't have to clean up the mess."

"Then?"

"I screamed, locked myself in the bathroom and swallowed a bottle of baby aspirin."

"That was sane?"

Madeline tilted her head. "Only six pills left. I take eight for a headache."

"Were you happy…before?"

Madeline furrowed her brow. "Yes…well…it wasn't perfect…."

"Ever try to make things better?"

She glowered at the woman. "I'm stuck with a two-year-old who blows lunch if he gets excited, a pair of twins who love to bite and a daughter who's either euphoric or threatening suicide, plus a Shih Tzu, that likes to urinate on anything leather."

"Have you discussed these problems with Ryan?"

Madeline bit her lip. "Late at night, when we were both tired? Working late – making love to his pretty girlfriend."

"And you felt?"

"Jealous. Why shouldn't I be?" She frowned. "Why am I telling you?"

"Because I'm here to help."

Madeline squinted. "What about the doctors?"

"Better not tell them much…or you could wind up as a permanent patient."

"I don't even know your name."

"Mrs. Docovitch." She reached into the drawer of her nightstand and brought out a purple box of talcum powder with a fluffy pink puff.

The soothing fragrance of lavender filled the room.

Mrs. Docovitch took the puff and taped some powder on her own neck then passed it over. "Here, try some."

Madeline sprinkled powder under her chin allowing some to fall under the neckline of her night dress. Taking a deep breath, her body relaxed. Madeline glanced down. "Powder's all over the floor. We're making lots of messy footprints."

Mrs. Docovitch laughed. "No worries. For what they charge – they'll clean our floor."

***

Ryan walked in, his suit wrinkled. "You look better."

"Having trouble with our little angels?"

Ryan coughed. "No…. Everything's under control."

Madeline's dimples showed. "I've decided to give you a divorce."

Ryan bounced in place. "I knew you'd come around."

"Jennifer should come to the house, get to know the kids."

"You wouldn't mind?"

"No."

"I'll give Jennifer the good news." He hurried out humming a tune.

"Why did you lie to him?" Mrs. Docovich asked.

"Lie? I believe Jennifer should get to know our children."

"You're very jealous."

31

"What's to be jealous of? She wears designer suits, silk blouses. After I outfit the kids, I'm lucky to have enough left of my allowance to buy a T-shirt."

Mrs. Docovich pointed to the wall. "Look in the mirror."

Madeline looked. "Ugh."

"What do you see?"

Madeline fluffed her hair. "A mess."

"I see a pretty woman. Why not brush your hair and apply a little make-up so the rest of the world would know? Your allowance – ever think of earning your own money?"

Madeline's unfocused eyes stared beyond the window. "I was a damn good journalist before I married."

"Aren't you the same person?"

"You're right. I still know a few people. I could even get a job."

Mrs. Docovich offered up the lavender powder to celebrate.

***

Ryan rushed his fingers through his hair. "I don't know how it happened. Jennifer's gone."

The corners of Madeline's mouth twitched. "That can't be true."

"Vickie ran in crying, locked herself in her room. The twins sat on Jennifer's lap, while she read them a story. Suddenly, they bit her on the face – both of them."

Madeline chomped on her fist to keep from laughing.

"Jennifer screamed, jumped up, the twins fell on the floor, howling, which woke the baby. Jenney rocked him and he vomited all over her new suit then Buster peed on her Gucci purse. She ran out screaming she never wanted to see me again."

Madeline snorted, her hand over her mouth.

"She couldn't handle the children for ten minutes while you…were always there."

Madeline's eyes sparkled.

"Do something different with your hair? Looks really pretty."

"Thanks. I've decided."

"Decided?"

"Yes. An old friend's an editor now, needs an assistant, she even offered me a place to stay till I get my own digs."

Ryan's eyes bulged. "What?"

"I leave here tomorrow and start work. You can have the house and the children. I won't need alimony."

"But you can't leave me."

"I'm not leaving you. You wanted a divorce. I agreed. I'll see the kids on weekends."

"But…."

"I'm happy. If it wasn't for you, I never would have straightened out my life."

32

"But the children?"

"You've a few days left, enough time to find a housekeeper."

Ryan dropped to his knees. "Madeline, I really love you."

"That's very flattering. Once I'm settled you can call me for a date. Now I must rest."

Ryan stood and shuffled out of the room mumbling to himself.

"How did I do?"

Mrs. Docovich winked. "You're on the road to recovery." She shared her lavender powder.

"Can I come back to see you?"

"Only if you're in trouble and need me."

***

Madeline entered her old room. She inclined her head at the cleaning lady. "Where's Mrs. Docovich?"

The lady stopped mopping. "Who?"

"Mrs. Docovich." Madeline pointed to the second bed.

"Ain't nobody been in that bed. You been patient here, in this room?"

"Yes."

"Five people came back looking for that Docovich lady. Hasn't been here for ten years."

Madeline smiled, remembering. "Only if I was in trouble, but things are fabulous." She left the cleaner to her work.

The woman frowned. "If they're crazy, why am I always mopping up two sets of footprints in all this perfumed powder?"

Michele Verbitski Knudsen grew up in New Jersey and came to Florida by way of Kansas City, but Florida's west coast captured her heart. Michele has a new romantic mystery series in the works and hopes both mystery lovers and romance aficionados will enjoy her unforgettable family of characters.

10. Marching Orders

My hospital room felt like a prison after the car crash. Might as well have bars and a guard.

"Push yourself, Kitten. Find your strength. Harkers never quit."

"Daddy, I can't. My legs won't move."

"Not acceptable. Use your mind. Hup one, hup two. Like I taught you when you were little. Lift those knees!"

I snapped "I'm not little. I'm trying my best."

"If you were trying your best you would be carrying your baton and leading the band."

I leaned on my metal crutches, willing my lifeless legs to obey. Their dead weight dragged down the lower half of my body. Sweat dripped in my eyes as I struggled and pushed. Nothing. I'd been trying for an hour to move an inch. My arms quivered. I was going to move my leg if I had to stay here all day. I bit down on my bottom lip, hard. Eyes squinched tight, my whole being focused on my stupid leg.

I felt a tiny, infinitesimal flutter below my knee. I looked down and saw the toe of my right shoe pushed out ahead of my left by an inch. "Daddy," I whispered, afraid I might have imagined it. "It moved."

"Not 'it' moved. You moved it. YOU."

"I did it."

"Didn't I tell you?" he said. "First step is always the hardest." I heard the grin in his voice, the pride.

That's all I needed. I loved making him proud. My rock, my coach, my cheerleader. No one had a better dad than me.

I closed my eyes and gripped the crutches tighter. One more inch would do me just fine.

For the next few weeks Dad showed up for every physical therapy session. Scolding, always pushing, shouting encouragement. We stayed after the physical therapist left to help other patients. He used his military voice to push me on. "Hup. One. Two. Three. That's it soldier. About time we got back in the race."

My shoulders ached. My neck cramped from holding up my head and my braces bit into my arms like they had teeth. But Harkers never quit. I sucked in another breath and gritted my teeth.

"That's my girl. We'll have you dancing in no time."

I sagged onto my crutches. "I'm so not a dancer, Dad. Maybe a marcher but not a dancer."

"Proud of you sweetheart. Remember when you were twelve, you got the most medals for perfect marching? Hell, you got a trophy for marching in the Rose Bowl."

"The whole band got the trophy, Dad. Not just me."

"Well, all I saw was you out there. You were always the best."

"That was a long time ago," I whispered and perched my chin on my crutch, swaying in place. A tiny rest on the way back to my room. "A long time ago." Tears burned my eyes. I felt them tickle my cheeks and let them drip. I needed both hands for my crutches.

"See you tomorrow baby." I felt him slap me on the butt. "You got this."

My favorite nurse came up behind me with a wheelchair. "I think you earned a ride. Hop in missy, I'm headed your way."

"No, I can make it." I eyed the wheelchair. "Oh, okay. Thanks." My sweat-soaked body collapsed onto the black vinyl seat.

"You're making great progress. Won't be long and you'll be out of here." She wheeled me to my bed and set the brake to help me stand.

"I can't wait," I panted. She stowed my crutches as I fell back on the pillows.

Three weeks later I was free of leg braces and using only crutches. I lied about my pain level so they'd release me. After Uber deposited me in front of my dorm, I stood wobbling on my crutches, wondering what to do next. At least they sent me home with pain meds. In what universe is being in pain and hobbling about on crutches healed? My universe.

I resumed my studies at the university and got special dispensation to continue my physical therapy at the campus medical center. Weeks passed, then months. I retired my crutches and though I walked on a cane with a limp Ahab might envy, at least I was walking.

But D-day—Drive Day—was approaching. I couldn't put it off any longer.

My car, newly repaired and shined up, waited for me in my parking space. I needed to get behind the wheel again, but the mere prospect made me cringe. The accident hadn't even been my fault. There I was, sitting in the left turn lane with my blinker on, when an idiot looked up from his iPhone just in time to plow into me.

I could do this. I needed to do this. Dad would be so proud when I walked up and showed him my progress. Yeah, maybe later. Suddenly, cleaning my room became all-important. Laundry morphed into a labor worthy of Hercules. And homework? Never had I been a more attentive student. Slipping my car key into the ignition would simply have to wait . . . until I ran out of excuses.

That day dawned clear, bright and sunny. Not a cloud in the sky. Not a raindrop in the forecast. Damn. No chance to use bad weather as my scapegoat.

I shuffled to the parking garage like approaching the gallows. My little, cheery royal blue Toyota had no sympathy for my impending doom. My hand shook so it took three tries to fit the key in the lock. I opened the door and tossed my cane into the front seat.

It took me five full minutes to crank the ignition.

My Corolla ignored the sweaty hands that gripped her steering wheel and started right up, settling immediately into her customary purr.

The drive to Dad's place occurred without mishap. I got up to speed in no time, actually tuned the radio like a normal person. Halfway there my heart slid from my throat back down to my chest where it belonged. And when I pulled to a stop at Dad's, I looked around and congratulated myself on this most glorious, gorgeous day.

The walk ahead would be no picnic. Grass lawns still gave me fits. But I couldn't let Dad see me struggle. The cane helped a lot there.

"Hey, Dad. Been awhile."

A mockingbird cheeped in a nearby tree as if scolding me.

"Thing is," I shifted feet, "I wanted to thank you for getting my ass moving. I couldn't have done it without you."

More cheeps. And a lawnmower off in the distance.

"You've always been there for me and, I'm sorry I haven't visited."

I leaned my cane against his headstone and dropped gingerly to the grass. It felt comfortable, familiar. The end date carved in granite stopped his life ten years ago. It never stopped our conversations.

I filled him in on schoolwork, college life, boys. "Miss you old man, but I've got to get back." I kissed his headstone. "I love you, Daddy."

I lurched back to the car. On the way, his voice counted cadence in my head.

One. Two.

I chuckled and straightened.

Lift the knees. Three. Four.

Frances Hight is an award-winning mystery/thriller writer with ties to critique groups in San Francisco and Orlando. She's a member of MWA and FWA, and a 2018 Royal Palm Literary Award Winner for her unpublished crime novel, Death of a Tomato. Her work has appeared multiple times in FWA Collections.

Turning Stones

When the Santa Ana winds howl in the deserts of southern California, they trigger sandstorms that erase footprints and strew garbage for miles. The rocky, sandy desert floor of the Coachella Valley, where my husband Michael and I are hunkered down, resembles a not-yet-tamed landfill in which garbage refuses to stay where people place it. Junipers, cacti, creosote, and withered grasses dot the miles and acres of this stark landscape.

I once heard a story of an elderly nun who traveled the country in an old bus with sisters from her order. Every time the bus stopped, the old woman jumped out and scurried to find a small stone, which she would either turn over or move a couple of inches. When asked about this odd behavior, she said, "I want to leave my mark, even if it's just in a small way."

I saw yet another way people leave marks as Michael and I drove the Alaskan Highway several years ago. When traveling in the RV, Michael generally drives while I make half-hearted attempts to navigate. More often though, I read, work Sudoku, or stare out the window in a vegetative trance.

It took four days of Alaskan Highway travel for my brain to register what my eyes had been blindly seeing. People had left messages along the highway by pulling over, picking up rocks, and rearranging them to spell things on the embankments. Once I noticed these configurations, I saw them everywhere.

"I'm seeing initials with either plus signs or hearts separating them," I said.

"Hometown and state names." Michael had slowed down, trying to read the messages as he drove. "Alma maters, college letters. Wow!" Occasionally, we would see spray-painted rocks, the letters jumping out for easy reading. Those painted rocks looked garish to me.

Michael suddenly slammed on the brakes and pulled off on the shoulder. "I've got to get a picture of this one." He grabbed his cell phone and hopped out of the RV. I followed.

He leaned over to frame the photo for the closest shot possible. "Be here now," the message read. "Very cool," Michael said. "Baba Ram Dass." Except we could no longer read the "now" part of the message. Ram Dass, known professionally as Richard Alpert, was a hip, Harvard-educated psychologist turn spiritualist from the sixties. Credited with helping to popularize Eastern religions and yoga in the United States, Ram Dass's book, Be Here Now, had been a Bible of sorts for Michael and me back in our early twenties.

Our progress along the Alaska Highway slowed considerably as my husband continued to stop for photographs. He wanted to make sure he got a representative sample of the messages.

"We've got to do this, too," he said. "I want us to leave a message."

The idea appealed to me in some ways. In other ways, not at all. "I need to think about it," I said. "What would you want to say?"

"Not sure. Guess I'll need to think about it, too."

We stopped at one point, got out of the RV, and walked up an embankment. I went so far as to pick up a rock. One rock. I could not make myself pick up a second one.

By the time we left The Yukon Territory, the topography had changed and we no longer saw hand-sized rocks along the shoulders. I was glad. Somehow, that raw and virginal terrain of northern Canada seemed too sacred to sully with a stupid rock arrangement. The Alaskan Highway had left a mark on me. I did not need to leave my mark on it.

What is it that compels us to want to leave our mark, whether it's initials carved on a picnic table, a message written with stones beside a highway, or a sliver of our soul we've revealed in a piece of writing? What drives us toward wanting to transcend our own mortality, to hope someone remembers us when we're gone? Could it be modern man's ethnocentric, arrogant belief that he is the center of the Universe, that time, history, and meaning do not exist outside his own lame and limited understandings?

Recently we visited the King Clone Ecological Reserve in the San Bernardino Mountains in Lucerne Valley, California. We drove for what felt like forever down single-lane roads with little traffic and only an occasional house to interrupt the vast high-desert expanse. Eventually we reached the Bessemer Mine Road, a passage so rough and gravelly we chose to leave the car beside the road. We walked the 1.3 miles to our destination, the home of an ancient ring of creosote bushes, *Larrea tridentata*. Scientists had carbon-dated the creosote King Clone root system at 11,700 years, suggesting it was perhaps the oldest living thing on the planet. Eleven thousand seven hundred years!

The California Fish and Game Commission had fenced off the Reserve with thin metal posts and two flimsy strands of wire. Only a cairn of small rocks about 18" high marked the spot where that incredible ring of creosote bushes had lived for almost 12,000 years, sending up new plants from the original centuries-old root system. Not a sign, not a marker, nothing but a few stakes in the ground where a fence had once circled the primordial specimen. Now the treasure sat unprotected and unmarked, vulnerable to all dangers that might come near, including the trampling footsteps of gawkers like me.

I stood in awe as I considered the age of those clones. I looked down and realized my footprints were like garbage, a tainting of something hallowed and sacred. I was thankful mine were not the only footprints surrounding the site.

Michael and I have been hiding almost four months already in this southern California desert. We've spent the past year seeking refuge from extreme weather, from metropolitan noise and congestion, but mainly from Covid-19. And while there are enough small rocks in this desert valley to leave many written messages, this area feels too holy to defile by rearranging a single stone. In the spots where the sand is loose rather than hard-packed, we leave behind our footprints. I'm reassured to know others will come behind us, destroy the impressions from our shoes, and leave their own. Eventually the frequent strong winds or the occasional torrential rains will erase every trace of every print. I feel a righteous relief to know I am not leaving behind any lasting marks.

Gerri Almand began writing humorous books when her excited husband convinced her they should buy an RV and travel the country. Their adventures led to The Reluctant RV Wife (2019) and Home Is Where the RV Is (2020). Running from Covid in our RV Cocoon is scheduled for release June, 2021.

Making Tracks

Let me tell you a story about how tracks are made. On a hot, breezy day, a small dinosaur crept along the edge of a salty lake. With a hunter's stealth, the little animal stepped slowly into the firm mud hoping to catch a lungfish at the water's edge. Yesterday, the waterline had been higher as the once large lake baked dry. Tomorrow, the shore would be another inch or two lower, hard as a rock, and already covered with a fine layer of ash-laden wind-blown sand. The evaporating lake was hunting grounds for this little dinosaur and also for large hungry crocodile ancestors that could be waiting in a wallow for any prey that ventured too close. We will never know who feasted on what or whom that day, just that the small dinosaur was there.

Eons later, in January 2021, a little girl scampering along the beach near Barry, Wales, realized the large chicken-like mark in the rock she found was something wonderful. She insisted her father snap a photo of it. When her parents sent the picture to the National Museum of Wales, scientists came immediately to retrieve the rock, delighted to study a fantastic prize—the clear footprint of a dinosaur. The three-toed animal was likely a 220-million-year-old Coelophysis, a surprise to the scientists who had never before found evidence of that animal in what is now Wales.

The recovery of such a find by a child was fabulous luck, but the survival of a footprint that ancient is also incredibly rare. Dinosaur footprints usually come in three different varieties. First is a cast, that is, the hardened sediment that filled the footprint, like someone would make a plaster mold today. Ancient casts don't age well and are often missing details. Next best are "underprints" which survive from dinosaurs so huge and heavy their steps crushed the soil beneath the print, accelerating preservation. A beach near Broome, Australia has a collection of these preserved in stone. And third and rarest is the true track like an imprint in the ground.

In defiance of all odds, the track in Wales was the third kind, so perfect even the claws on the toe tips and the depth of the footpads stood out clearly. If the animal was indeed a Coelophysis, it was about three feet high at the shoulder and six feet long. An early, "economy" version of a T-rex, it walked on two hind legs, used short front legs and claws to grasp, ate with a long narrow snout of sharp teeth, and balanced with a three-foot whip-like tail. Before this Welsh track turned up, the United States and Southern Africa were the only places this early dinosaur had been found.

We human beings know all about preserved footprints. In neighborhoods across America, many concrete sidewalks and driveways have a shoeprint, handprint, or even a name intentionally etched in them. A dog, cat, bird or even a deer might have accidentally left a mark, too. Dinosaurs didn't have the advantage of concrete. They lived in a natural world where footprints were made in mud. So, how in this world did dinosaur tracks ever endure for eons?

When I did a quick Google search of "how do dinosaur tracks survive," I found an interesting video by a paleontologist. In a charming Australian accent, the scientist provided a sound explanation of how ancient footprints were preserved, but at the end, he admitted that nobody really knows by what "magic" these marks survive. Let's just call it astronomically good luck.

After all, footprints are usually ephemeral. If we track mud, sand, or grass across our floors, we remove the offending footwear, clean up the mess, and afterward, install a boot tray near the door where shoes and boots can be left. (The Japanese have been leaving their footwear at the door for centuries.) If someone is being tracked by their footprints, it has to be done quickly before something—the elements or another heavy-footed creature—obscures the prints. American Indian trackers known for their skill often use the most transitory signs, such as newly broken foliage, misplaced gravel at a stream's edge, a small patch of flattened grass. In the case of the Welsh seacoast footprints, they could only have been saved by the confluence of the perfect ingredients.

The scenario I created at the beginning accounted for tracks in mud, but not just any old wet ground would do. Modern-day cattle and horses often leave prints preserved in dried up mud along streambanks, but those tracks only last until the next rain and another trampling by the same thirsty animals. So, the footprint-preserving ground must have also contained a hardening agent.

Concrete is a mixture of stones and soil held together by a natural binder, cement. The Romans developed a foolproof concrete recipe of clay laced with broken and pulverized seashells (limestone) and sand mixed with volcanic ash. "Roman concrete" was so durable it can still be found in Roman structures dotting the Italian countryside and even around dock pilings at ancient Mediterranean seaports. Two thousand years later, none of those artifacts show much wear.

So, the Welsh dinosaur must have walked in the perfect mix of gravel-laced clay mud, pulverized seashells, and sandy volcanic ash in a hot, parching climate. The hardened tracks were gradually covered with layer upon layer of silt as the salty lake swelled with rain, then shrunk under the baking sun. Millions of years of continental drift buried the solidified, silt-covered tracks until the Atlantic Ocean's pounding waves eroded the Welsh rock layers above them.

The "magical" survival of these tracks makes me wonder about the ones I might leave behind. If my shoe prints were somehow found in high-grade concrete a mere hundred thousand years from now, what would the finder think she had found? Would she know that the track was a covering for my foot, complete with the emblem of the shoemaker stamped into the concrete? Or would she and her scientific colleagues divide us into subspecies based on the brand of shoes we wore? "These are the 'adidasians' with many square pads on the end of their appendage and grooves toward the back, whereas the 'skechersians' had small square pads over the whole foot. We aren't sure if they were separate species or were able to interbreed."

If our eons-distant relatives or some creatures from another star system actually thought shoe prints were feet, what would they think of the even more rare barefoot print? "We don't know what to make of the smooth tracks with five oval digits at the top. This must have been a different species of human, one more agile than the skechersians." And what of a handprint? Would the beings who found it say to each other, "Was there ever a 'human' that walked on feet with small, square footpads and long, slender extensions allowing it to grasp and climb? Perhaps, they climbed the tall structures and lived in them."

If they knew so little about us, would they ever be able to decipher "Sarah (heart with an arrow) Harry?"

Lynn Bechdolt is a retired pastor who has lived in several states before moving to Florida to be near her family. She arrived with a red Boston terrier named Scarlet who keeps her honest about the promises she makes.

Footprints in the Snow

"Shoot," his father whispered lying beside him.

Phillip had the majestic ten-point buck in his sites, but didn't pull the trigger.

"Shoot him," his father urged again, but Phillip couldn't do it. The animal lifted his head, looked right at Phillip, and ran off.

"You had him, Phillip. That's the one everyone is after." His father got up, brushed the snow off his clothes and stared at his twelve-year-old son still lying motionless on the ground. "Well, get up. He's headed for the woods. We'll try to catch him by taking a short cut across the field. He didn't hear a shot, so he may not be spooked."

Phillip was so excited when the day started. He followed his father across the snowy terrain, emulating his walk, how he carried his gun, even stepping in his footprints. For several weeks, Phillip's father had been preparing him for his first hunt, buying him a new rifle and hunting jacket, and telling him stories about how he and Phillip's grandfather used to hunt together.

"I got a buck my first day of hunting," his father reminisced, "and my father was so proud, but I was lucky, so don't expect to even see a big one the first day."

But they did see a big one, and instead of making his father proud, Phillip froze. He just wasn't expecting the buck to look so majestic, so powerful.

Neither said anything as they trudged across the snowy field in a single file with Phillip still trying to match his father's footprints and worried that his father was disappointed in him. After fifteen minutes Phillip broke the silence. "Dad, I'm sorry I couldn't shoot him."

"Well, lots of people have trouble killing their first deer. They call it deer fever." Phillip's father said as he kept walking.

"He wasn't just an ordinary buck, Dad." Phillip moved closer to his father.

"Right, he was a ten-point buck. You don't see those everyday."

"He was beautiful. Didn't you ever feel that something was too beautiful to kill?"

Footprints

"You have to remember, they're animals, and we're hunters." Phillip's father glanced back at his son. "Man has always hunted."

"But it's different if you hunt to eat."

"We are going to eat it."

"Mom doesn't like deer meat."

"You eat bacon and steak, don't you?"

"Yeah"

"Where do think they come from? Someone had to kill cattle and pigs."

Phillip continued silently for a moment. "I just never thought eating meat was like killing an animal."

Phillip's father stopped and faced his son. "Think of hunting like culling the herd, making room for the younger males. When deer get overpopulated, they start to starve to death. That buck would rather be shot than starve to death. So do you want to go on?"

Phillip wasn't sure he wanted to go on, but he couldn't quit now after all the preparation. He wanted to be like his father. It was bad enough that he didn't make the football team. He couldn't fail at hunting too. Besides, they probably wouldn't see another deer.

"No, let's go on, and if we see him again, I'll shoot him," Phillip said, but secretly he hoped the buck was long gone.

Phillip's father turned and continued at a faster pace. Phillip, still trying to follow in his father's footsteps whenever he could, had trouble keeping up. Several minutes later, his father stopped and took out his binoculars. "We're in luck. He's there, right before the woods, and he has a doe and fawn with him. Look."

Phillip took the binoculars and saw the buck as regal as before. The doe and fawn made him think of his own family.

"It will be hard to hit him from here," his father said. "We'll get closer, but we don't want him to pick up our scent. Let's walk to that single tree over there."

Phillip's heart sank as they made their way to the tree. When they got there, his father took out his binoculars again. "He's still there, and so are the doe and the fawn. You don't want to hit them. You only get one deer for the season. Make sure you aim for the buck's shoulder so you get the heart with one shot. You don't just want to wound him."

Phillip leaned against the tree, sighted-in his rifle, and aimed at the buck's shoulder. He knew a wounded buck might run for miles before he dropped. Carefully, Phillip aimed, and pulled the trigger, all the while telling himself he didn't want to make the animal suffer.

The shot was perfect, and the buck dropped. The female took off, but the fawn froze, sniffed the buck and then took off too.

"You got him," Phillip's father yelled and ran toward the downed buck. Phillip just stood where he was, tears filling his eyes.

"Come on, Phillip," his father yelled running across the field. Even his footprints with their long strides looked happy.

Phillip wasn't happy, and he slowly trudged across the field to where the buck lay in the snow, a small puddle of red blood next to the wound. Glassy eyes stared up at Phillip.

"This is the biggest I've seen," his father said. "He is a beauty. I bet the Rod and Gun Club will want to mount his head for the clubhouse. He's bigger than the one they have there now." His father walked around the buck surveying its size. "We have to get a picture of you with it" His father pulled out his phone. "Crouch down and get in there."

"No, I don't want a picture," Phillip said wiping a tear from his cheek.

Surprised by his response, Phillip's father looked over at his son, and for the first time noticed that Phillip was crying.

"What's wrong?" Phillip's father asked.

Phillip wasn't sure how to answer and looked out over the field where two sets of very different footprints led to the downed buck. More than anything, he had wanted to be like his father and make his father proud of him. Though his father was proud and happy, Phillip felt like a miserable failure.

"I wish I had had the courage not to shoot," Phillip said.

As his father absorbed what his son said, the excitement drained from his face. He walked over to Phillip and put his arms around him. "Oh, Phillip," he said and held his son.

"I just didn't want to disappoint you," Phillip mumbled into his father's shoulder.

"Hunting's not for everyone," his father said patting Phillip on the back. "Let's go home."

They walked through the snow side by side to get the truck and bring the buck home. Phillip never went hunting again, but he never forgot the magnificent buck that didn't deserve to die.

In the years to come, whenever he saw footprints in fresh snow, he thought of that day. It was the day he realized that he and his father didn't need to agree on everything, and he didn't need to follow in his father's footprints. He had to forge his own path.

Monica Becker is a former college professor who has authored many research articles, but since she retired, she has concentrated on fiction writing. She has published in eight FWA Collections, placed in writing competitions, and made the RPLA finals list numerous times. She resides with her husband in Venice, Florida.

I Heard Footprints

"Dad." Her voice, far away, yet distinct. "Dad." More insistent, small and barely above a whisper.

My feet absorbed the floor's night cold and sent a chill to the base of my neck. The door to her bedroom was ajar and I gently pushed it open. "Hey, Cat. What is it?"

She sat cross-legged in the center of her bed, hands clasped in her lap. Shadows played across her face, evoking a sadness that belied her twelve years. "I heard footprints."

A cold shudder streaked across my shoulders when I reached for her hand "It's okay. You had a bad dream. Miss Mom?"

Cat shrugged at our reflected images on the dark window pane. "Yeah, I guess so."

Cat's mother, Jenna, called three days before to say she was still caring for her ailing mother and didn't know when she would return. I reasoned that must be the cause of Cat's restlessness and nightmares.

"I didn't hear anything, but I'll check the house, if it will make you feel better."

"Okay." She snuggled under the flowered bedspread. Her hair, the color of wildflower honey, framed her face.

My lungs filled with the soothing scent of lavender but my eyes stung when I realized that this sweet, innocent, child would too soon shoulder the fears, doubts, and worries that come with being a woman.

"Go back to sleep and don't worry about hearing footsteps."

Her eyes fixed on mine with an intensity she inherited from her mother.

"I heard footprints. Not footsteps." Her voice dripped with pre-teen exasperation.

Back off. Don't push. Footsteps, footprints, it doesn't matter. Calm her down.

"If you say you heard footprints, then that's what you heard. We can talk about it in the morning." I kissed her forehead. "Now, go back to sleep."

She turned on her side and nodded to blackness beyond the window. "I did hear them. They tinkled."

47

Footprints

***

Bacon and coffee aromas mingled as I whisked pancake batter the next morning. Cat slipped into her chair without acknowledging my presence. "Good morning sunshine. Sleep well?"

"I guess so." She flicked through her phone.

"You had a bad dream. You okay?"

"I'm fine."

A brief sizzle rose from the griddle as the pancake batter spread into disks. "I want to make sure you understand what you said last night. Remember, you can't hear footprints, you can only see footprints. You hear footsteps."

"Whatever." Flick, flick. "But I heard them."

I poked at the edges of the pancakes, hoping the right words would rise from the steam. Ah, hell. Just go for it.

I angled the spatula under the edge of a pancake to test its doneness. "Mom called me this morning. Grandma passed away last night."

Her finger stopped in mid-flick. "Oh. Okay."

Two pancakes and a strip of bacon slid onto Cat's plate. "You don't seem upset about Grandma."

"It's sad. But I knew it was her time to go."

My face pinched and my eyes narrowed. "What do you mean?"

"The footprints, remember? I heard them last night."

Her attitude and tone bristled my neck hairs. "How many times do I have to say it, you can't hear footprints. You can only see footprints. Did you hear footsteps?"

Cat gently set her phone next to her plate. Her hazel eyes projected calm and peacefulness. "I guess so." She shoved a forkful of pancake into her mouth. "Good pancakes, Dad. You wanna make breakfast every day?"

Like the butter atop my pancake stack, annoyance melted. "Looks like that's what I'll be doing for a while." I scooted my chair closer to the table. Morning pancakes made everything all right. "Hey, sorry I snapped at you."

"No prob. When I heard the footprints, I knew it was Grandma. So, I wasn't surprised when you told me."

"Whoa. You knew Grandma died?"

"Yeah. It's the same with Toby and old Mrs. Michaelson."

Two years ago, we lost Toby, the terrier adopted a year after Cat was born. I rechewed a mouthful of pancake. Our elderly neighbor, Mrs. Michaelson, died last year. "You saw footprints when they died?"

"No, I heard footprints. Remember?"

"Oh, right. You heard footprints."

Let it go. So, she hears footprints. That's not so bad.

***

Footprints

The EMTs found Jenna and Cat holding hands in the wreckage. They were returning from Cat's college in another state. Rain-slick roads and a drunken driver running a red light were ascribed as the causes of the crash that snuffed out Jenna's life. But Cat only suffered a severe bump on the head.

Two days after letting go of Jenna, a sob welled up in my chest when I took Cat's hand in the hospital.

"How are you feeling, Cat?"

"Okay, I guess. My head hurts. Dry throat."

I poured water into a plastic cup. "Mom is gone." My hand shook as I held the cup with its bent straw close to Cat's mouth.

A tear trickled along her temple and disappeared into her hair, aged now to a light henna. "I figured as much. I heard the footprints."

"Cat, you know better. You can't hear footprints. You can see them, but not hear them."

"I heard them. Faintly. Like those Buddhist monk's bells. And I saw them this time. Glowing footprints that disappeared when the bells faded."

"You must have been dreaming. They said you were unconscious. Thank God, you only have a concussion.

"I didn't dream it, Dad. Mom told me she heard footprints, too."

"Mom heard footprints?"

"She said she heard them her whole life, right before someone died. But she never told anyone."

The plastic cup rattled when I placed it on the tray. "Okay. You heard the footprints. We don't have to talk about it now. The doctors said we can go home tomorrow. Now get some rest. I'll see you in the morning."

***

Warm pressure on my hand dissolved the last wisps of an unrecoverable dream. My eyes blinked open to a hovering woman. Humming, beeping machines brought me back to my hospital bed.

"Hey, Dad. It's Catherine. Can you hear me?"

My chin dipped, rubbing a plastic face mask against my beard.

"Good. Don't try and talk. I couldn't hear you anyway with all these monitors."

That smile. The tilt of her head. Sunlight peeking through her hair. Is it Cat? Maybe it's Jenna.

"I'm glad you're awake. I wanted to tell you that it's all right. You can let go."

My hand squeezed into the warmth.

"I heard the footprints last night. Give Mom my love when you see her." She kissed my forehead and slipped from my field of vision, giving me permission to close my eyes against the sunlight. A ripple of hushed voices

49

washed over me. I sucked air from the mask but it grated against the back of my throat.

***

Running through a forest, I could feel my feet thumping on the trail. My eyes focused on footprints in the muddy track. Each stride drew me nearer to tinkling bells. Cat. I hear them. The footprints. I hear the footprints.

William Clapper is a Bradenton-based former journalist who writes about ordinary people in everyday situations. His fiction has appeared in FWA's annual Collection and The Florida Writer magazine. His non-fiction writings were featured in magazines, newspapers, websites and more recently, in association and organization newsletters.

A Hill of Courage

I usually leave my bungalow at 5:30 in the morning. and walk to my office at the high school. In the Congo, because of the heat, school begins at sunup and ends at noon. Lately, I had been noticing unusual marks on the path leading up to the elementary and high schools. They were deep, square imprints all along the sandy-clay path.

Valerie, one of our high school teachers caught up with me and I asked her about the strange markings on the ground.

"Oh, that's Antionette," she told me.

"She must wear unusual shoes to make a print like that."

"I'll show you at noon when the children walk home."

"Just tell me, Valerie."

"No, you have to see for yourself."

"Very well. At noon then."

She nodded and headed toward her high school classroom.

My curiosity had really been growing but now it peaked. What was so unusual about this girl Antionette's shoes that would make marks like that?

When the noon bell rang at both schools, I locked my principal's office, the teacher's lounge, and headed home. Valerie met me and we made our way toward the long line of small children heading down the hill to their village.

"Let's wait under the big mango," she said. The shade of the large, old tree served as the place for the school market where roasted peanuts and small rolls of fresh bread could be purchased.

As we shared a small paper cone of warm peanuts, the children were thinning out. We moved away from the tree and were almost to the path when I saw her. Her legs were shriveled and she had her school books strapped to her back. Her clothes were in tatters and she literally had to drag herself everywhere she went. Each hand held a solid square wooden block which she used to pull herself along.

"It's not possible," I whispered. "Won't anyone help her? Why doesn't she have a wheelchair?"

"She doesn't ask for help. Never has. She's been pulling herself up and down the hill for seven or eight years, one of the teachers told me."

"Why haven't I seen her in all that time?"

51

Valerie stopped and shook her head. "You wouldn't see her because she leaves the village each morning at four o'clock, while everyone is still sleeping. I would think she would pass by your house maybe by five. You're just getting up."

I was frozen on the path. The image of Antoinette so infuriated me I grabbed Valerie's arm and said, "Come on."

"Where are we going?

"You'll see."

We rushed past the few remaining children on the path to my house. I ran inside, grabbed the keys to the Jeep and motioned for Valerie to get in. Backing out, I swung onto the grass that ran along the path to the school. When we got to the end where the crippled child was slowly making her way, I stopped and jumped out. Valerie followed me.

"Antoinette," I said as kindly as I could, "Do you know who I am?"

"Yes, Sir."

"I want to give you a ride home in my Jeep. Will you allow me to help you?"

The child had a beautiful face, perfectly proportioned and eyes that grabbed my soul.

"I don't know, Sir. If you want to, I guess it's okay."

"Help me, Valerie," I said. We lifted the girl easily and placed her on the front seat across from me. Valerie jumped into the seat behind.

"I've never been in a car before," Antoinette said.

"You'll have to show me where you live. Can you do that?" I asked.

She nodded as I started down the dirt road. We quickly caught up with the last of the elementary students and flew past them. Everyone stopped to stare at who was sitting in the front seat. Shouts of "Antoinette!" could be heard above the roar of the Jeep's motor.

She laughed. "I'll be home before they will," she said, a large grin on her face.

Nsaya was a small village of perhaps three-hundred inhabitants. Two other villages beyond could be seen from the road as we descended the steep hill.

"It's over there, Sir," she said, pointing to a small mud hut with a straw roof. A small black dog barked at us as we pulled to a stop in front.

Valerie helped me lift the girl out of the Jeep.

"Thank you for bringing me home. I beat everyone!"

"Yes, you did," I said. "Now I want you to listen to me very carefully. Do you have an alarm clock?" She nodded and I continued. "Good. Set it for 5 o'clock and get ready for school as you always do. I'll be here with the Jeep at 5:30 and we'll go to school together."

The girl began to shake her head. "Oh, no, I can't do that. Everyone will be so jealous."

I scowled. "Let me worry about them. You just be ready at 5:30. Do you agree?"

She nodded, and Valerie and I hopped into the car, turned around and headed back up to the mission station.

We didn't talk because the motor made such a racket climbing the steep hill. When I pulled back into the driveway, I stopped and turned off the motor.

"Do you mean you're going to pick up that girl every morning from now on?"

"Yes, I am. When I saw her for the first time I became so angry I didn't know what I was going to do. Now I do. You know how these people mistreat anything weak or injured."

Valerie nodded. "Yes, and it's a shame."

"Maybe I can show them a better way," I said.

For the next month, the 'Antoinette parade' had everyone crowding around the Jeep and cheering as we pulled up in front of the elementary school. Through friends at the U.S. embassy we were able to find a used motorized wheelchair, and one of the Peace Corps workers helped find new clothes and a desk for the girl's house.

Over the next few years, Antoinette was admitted to high school and finished with honors. Through assistance from the American Hospital, she received the latest surgical procedures and braces which allowed her to stand. She graduated from the Provincial Teacher Training school and is now a teacher at the school she attended.

At an honored place on a shelf behind my desk sit two, square wooden blocks, the gift of a child who'd imprinted my heart forever.

 **William G. Collins** loves history and has written and published forty-two novels, many are mysteries set in Ancient Egypt. He is a co-leader of the Port Orange Scribes and has two books coming out in May. One is about traveling back in time.

After You

the pine you slashed, bleeds
I dip a finger into sap—taste

the sweetness hits first, then the tang
knifing up through nasal passages
the quick breath—sharp
oh yes, you've come this way

I kneel
run a finger over the scar
your shoe made in the mud
a disfigurement recognizable
by the ridging on the right
deeper there—those shoes
laced tight for lashing out

farther on
a young willow, slender branched
but crippled—the bent limb
yet another sign of your trespass

yes—I'm here, again,
trailing you through the scrublands
bandaging the wounded
wondering what door you jimmied
to escape and machete through my memory

Shutta Crum has written poems that have appeared in *Typehouse, Stoneboat, Southern Poetry Review* and *Beyond Words*. Forthcoming: *Main Street Rag*. She was nominated for a Pushcart Prize by *Typehouse*. Her chapbook *When You Get Here* (2020) won a gold RPLA. Her book, *THUNDER-BOOMER!* was a *Smithsonian* magazine and ALA notable book. www.shutta.com.

The Last Dance

"Thanks for coming, Marco," Anna says.

"You should have called me sooner."

"He didn't want you to come. You know your brother, this has to be done his way."

"How bad is he?"

"Weeks, maybe days. Each time I see him, he's more frail."

"Why is he at the beach house? Shouldn't he be here where you, or someone, can care for him?"

"I tried, but he doesn't want to be a burden, especially to his ex-wife. He's forty-five years old, and he's acting like a petulant child! This is why he divorced me, you know?"

"I thought you both—"

"No. I didn't understand, at the time, but the whole thing was a sham to set me free. He got the diagnosis and filed for divorce two weeks later. He never told me, Marco, I swear. I would have stayed."

"Did you tell him I was coming?"

She looks down, "No. I was afraid he'd try to stop you.

Marco shakes his head, "He doesn't want to need you or me or anyone else. He's been like that since our Dad left. Artie was only fifteen, but he stepped up for Mom and me. He was nine years older, and he taught me all I know about life. He always told me to remember that whatever we do, wherever we go, we leave traces behind like footprints that prove we were there. So we should do right.

"I grew up trying to follow the footprints he left behind. In school, I took the same classes, played the same sports. I became a musician to be like him. I only married Stephanie because he married you.

"I did it all to earn his love, but I realized it wasn't fair to Stephanie. When I came out, I told him first, even before I told my wife. If I had known how he'd react, I would have—hell, I don't know what I would have done."

Anna rests her hand on his arm, "Don't blame yourself. He never should have cut you out of his life. Gay or straight, you're still his little brother."

Marco smiles, "I wish he could see it that way. It's late. I'll go out there first thing in the morning. Thanks, Anna, you're the best. Most ex-wives wouldn't put up with all this."

"Ironic, isn't it? It took a divorce and a death sentence to make me realize how much I still love him. I'd give anything to be with him for these last days."

***

Bonita Cove is one of a thousand inlets carved out of the California coastline by the relentless Pacific. At low tide, a thin stretch of sand emerges at the base of the rocks, only to disappear hours later when the sea returns.

Marco takes a long look at the ocean, then enters the beach house. A young man in blue scrubs meets him at the door.

"You must be Marco. I'm your brother's aide, Terry. Anna told me to expect you."

"How is he today?"

"He's resting now, poor dear. He had a tough night. I didn't tell him you were coming, but I cleaned him up for you, like Anna said. I'll be right here, if you need me."

Marco walks toward the bedroom, but the sight of his emaciated brother stops him in the doorway.

Artie scoffs, "Judging by your expression, I must look even worse than I think!"

"Hey, Artie. No, you—"

"Don't bother lying. I know what I look like. What are you doing here? Did she call you? I told her—"

"Of course, she called me! It's what family does. They call on each other when things get tough."

"I don't need you here. I can deal with this on my own."

"C'mon, Artie. For God's sake, this isn't the time."

"Why—because I'm dying? So what? We're supposed to pretend we get along just because the end is near? What's the point?"

"Maybe there is no point for you, but what about Anna? What about me? We're the only ones left to mourn for you and, like it or not, we love you. You don't have to love us back, but you don't have to be such an ass, either."

Artie is slow to respond, "Is that any way to talk to a dying man?"
Marco pulls a chair next to the bed.

"Before you sit, open the curtains, will you? That view never gets old."
Marco pulls back the drapes, "It is spectacular."

"It's more than that—it's eternal. The ocean goes on forever."

"I can understand why you want to be here."

"How is Anna?"

"She's a trooper, Artie, but she's hurting. She wants to be here, with you. Let me call her, please."

Artie opens his mouth but chokes on his words, coughing and gagging as his body convulses. Terry appears by the bed, turns him on his side and elevates his head. In moments, the coughing subsides.

Artie locks his eyes on his brother and whispers, "Call her."

Marco sits with him all day and they talk about old times. Anna brings supper. They set Artie's wheelchair on the porch, overlooking the cove and balance plates of Anna's pasta de pepe. Artie only picks at his meal, but the others pretend not to notice.

When the sun has set, Terry points to the cove, "What is that?"

Blue-green light glows in each breaking wave like liquid bands of neon.

"Noctiluca!" Marco says. "Bioluminescent algae. It's been years since I've seen it."

Artie smiles, "Remember that night—after Mom's funeral? We sat right here, drinking wine and telling stories."

"I remember. When the noctiluca appeared, we went down to the beach. Each step we took kicked up sparks in the sand. It was like walking on stars! You danced around like Zorba the Greek."

"You did too!"

"No—I just stepped in your footprints. That's the story of my life, Artie—stepping where you step, going where you go. I always wanted to be you."

Artie's eyes glisten, "I should've—when you told me—I should've," he sighs. "I'm sorry, Marco. You deserve better."

"So do you, brother. So do you."

A moment later Marco says, "Let's go! One last dance on the stars."

"I can't."

"Sure, you can—we'll help."

Marco, Anna and Terry muscle Artie's wheelchair down the path to the beach. The waves glow and the sand sparkles with each step.

Marco tries spinning Artie's chair around, but the wheels sink in the sand.

"C'mon, brother. All those years you carried me, now it's my turn to carry you."

Marco lifts Artie, piggy-back style, surprised by how little he weighs. Slowly he dances a circle around Anna, the sand like sparklers flashing at his feet.

Artie cries, "YES! YES!".

They walk along the water's edge, leaving a trail of footprints in the wet sand, until Artie rasps, "Enough, little brother. You've carried me far enough."

Marco turns around and sees the incoming tide washing away their footprints. As the last one disappears, he feels Artie's breathing slow and his arms go limp around his shoulders.

Marco knows without looking. The last dance is over.

William Delia is a storyteller in prose, poetry and song. The characters in his stories reach for something more in life, even as they struggle with life's everyday challenges. Delia lives and writes in Central Florida.

The Library Steps

Sitting alone at the end of Willow Road only blocks from the historic center of what Google told us was one of the top ten best small towns in America, the house looked like a well-maintained version of Norman Bates house in the film Psycho. I encouraged my friends to read Robert Bloch's 1959 novel after they'd watched the movie. But I guess that's the librarian in me.

We came to Vermont to escape the craziness of the past year. The realtor had shown us the home on a lark. She said it had sat empty since the last owners unexpectedly left town and made a joke about how they were anxious to sell. When I asked why they left, she laughed nervously and said, "Some people think the house is haunted, but that's just twaddle."

"Twaddle?" Mark's eyebrows went up. Mark can rattle off esoteric computer programming language that leaves me baffled, but twaddle isn't in his vocabulary.

Neither of us believed in ghosts and we instantly fell in love with the house with its mix of Victorian architecture and more contemporary upgrades throughout the house. But it was the library that sold me. I loved the dark wood paneling and shelving that climbed to the high ceiling. It even had a rolling ladder to reach the top shelves.

We spent the next two months unpacking, moving furniture, and turning the old house into our home. The library became my pet project and my office space. The hardwood floors gleamed after I cleaned and waxed them, and I spent days shelving books.

Mark took a break from his computer one afternoon and found me staring at the last unopened box. The words Photo Albums were scribbled across the top in black Magic Marker.

"Are you okay, hon?" he said, slipping a comforting arm around me.

I nodded.

"Do you want my help?"

I shook my head, turned, and kissed him on the cheek. "Thanks, but I've got this. Why don't you make us a couple of grilled cheese sandwiches and I'll join you in a few minutes?"

The days slipped by, moving into a summer the locals told us was inordinately warm, followed by a blast of color in the fall when the leaves turned, and the temperature dropped into the 40s.

Maybe it was the cold weather that brought him inside because that's the first time I saw the footprints on the polished library floor. Six small footprints. They appeared to have entered from the French doors leading to the backyard and taken six steps into the room before fading away.

No one had been in this room except the two of us, and these were not the prints of two fully grown adults. I might have overlooked them if the sun hadn't blazed through the French doors and splashed across the floor. Looking closely, I could see the sole's waffle design and was sure they belonged to a pair of Van's.

Using my best Sherlock Holmes deductive reasoning, I surmised that whoever had left the prints had walked through the back garden, stepping in the loamy, acidic soil, and entered through the French doors. I moved to the doors and pulled on the handle. Locked. This made no sense, and then I remembered what the realtor had told us: "Some people think the house is haunted, but that's just twaddle."

Twaddle? Maybe, but how to explain these prints appearing out of nowhere and disappearing? Mark was in the middle of a major project, and I didn't want to bother him with what might have simply been vestigial markings from the previous owners' children. Perhaps I hadn't done as good a job cleaning and polishing the hardwood as I thought.

I marched to the kitchen and returned with a damp mop and a few dry rags. Within minutes the floor was spotless. The footprints were gone, but not the puzzle.

Temperatures dropped even more the next week, but sunlight dappled off the creek at the bottom of the hill behind the house. I pulled Mark away from his computers and convinced him to take advantage of the cold but dazzling Vermont day. Bundled in our winter parkas with wool caps and gloves, we looked like we were preparing for an Arctic adventure, but we laughed together, seemingly for the first time in a long time, as we hiked through the woods and along the creek.

Back at the house, I made a pot of tea and took my cup to the library to work on my journal. I'd only taken a few steps into the room when I saw them. Six more footprints, made by the same boy's sneakers. They appeared to have started, not at the French doors this time, but from where the last ones had ended. The six prints stopped about twelve feet from the bookshelves on the far wall of the library.

Something caught in my throat and I swallowed hard. Was the house truly haunted? Could I be imagining these ghostly footsteps? I lowered myself to my knees next to the prints and studied them for a long moment. Each one was well defined enough, although they faded away on the edges, but it was unquestionably not my imagination. I extended a shaking finger and ran it across the heel section of the closest print. Gritty specks of sand clung to my finger. At least I wasn't going crazy.

I didn't know where this was leading, but I did know there had to be a rational explanation and I was determined to ferret out the answer on my own. Only when I solved the puzzle would I tell Mark since he wouldn't believe me otherwise.

There were no footprints for the next three weeks, and I thought it might have all ended. But on October 9, a day that had dawned dark and gloomy, shrouding the house in shadows and filling me with feelings of doom, the footprints were back. Maybe it was the depressive nature of that day, but I screamed when I saw the six footprints ending at the bookcase.

"What's wrong?" Mark screamed as he hurried into the library.

I pointed at the footprints. "They keep coming back," I stammered.

Mark gazed at the prints then at me. His eyes shone. His hands shook. "Oh, honey. I'm so sorry." And then he cradled me in his arms.

"I can't get rid of them," I said. "I wash them off and they come back."

"I know. I know."

Eyes glistening with tears, he followed the track of the footprints to the bookshelf. Reaching up to a higher shelf he pulled down one of the photo albums and opened it to a tear-stained page filled with glossy prints of a happy family. Two loving parents and a smiling six-year-old boy wearing high-topped Van's sneakers.

"Baby," Mark said softly. "It's been a year, but Bobby will always be a part of us. We can't replace him, but we can move on, like those footprints. Maybe it's time to try once more."

He hugged me again before replacing the photo album next to the pair of Bobby's sneakers.

Victor DiGenti is an award-winning author and publisher. He's penned six novels and six works of nonfiction. He's a longtime FWA member, a former Executive VP and conference faculty chair.

Footprints at the Edge

The most rational of men, Josh Rowbotham founded an entirely new scientific field, which he named "Astro-Biochemistry." When *Astronomy* magazine, in a four-page puff piece complete with photos of Josh and his lab, asked him to describe Astro-Biochemistry, he poetically responded, "Seeking the footprints of life at the edge of the universe."

Josh used telescope spectroscopy to identify the building blocks of life on exoplanets revolving distant stars. He observed light shifts occurring billions of years ago, signs of the joining of elements into chemicals, some of which had the potential to become the precursors of life. No hand of God was present in his spectral analyses, just the logical combinations of atoms into molecules, and molecules into larger and more complex molecules. Life was out there on billions of planets, skeptics be damned.

Josh, an unmarried man with little concern for his appearance, resided in a small house in Pasadena and he taught at Cal Tech. Adventure for Josh involved spending time at the viewfinders of telescopes in California, Hawaii, and Chile. Vacation, after thirty-four years at the university, was taking a few days off to relax following long nights on the telescopes before heading to a different observatory or back to his lab. So, there was surprise all around when he told the administration and his grad students he would be taking two weeks off to observe a solar eclipse from aboard a small cruise ship in the middle of the South Pacific.

Sky & Telescope magazine had chartered the MV Amundsen and sold tickets at over five-thousand dollars per passenger, telescopes included. Josh travelled free in exchange for a one-hour lecture on Astro-Biochemistry presented to his fellow passengers.

His public, non-scientific lectures always began "Look up into the night sky and see those billions of twinkling points of light." A picture of galaxies spread across a field of inky blackness appeared on the projector screen. "Each tiny dot is a massive sphere of gas…" and here a pulsing, boiling ball of orange and yellow was seen, "… and has, on average, seven orbs circling at any point in time." Globes of rock were shown in a variety of colors circling the gaseous sphere. "And on any of those orbiting balls of rock and gas, the chemicals for creating life may be present, whether within a primordial soup, evolved into fully sentient beings, or something in-between." A bubbling cauldron of volcanic ooze would appear, then Professor Rowbotham was off and running on his favorite topic.

The cruise left Oahu in a south-westerly direction on October 17th, three days before the eclipse.

There were no observers when the block-long, ink-black submarine surfaced under the Amundsen on the moonless night of October 19th, breaking the cruise ship's keel with a resounding scream of metal, sending it plummeting to the Pacific depths. Josh, one of a handful of people using the telescopes on deck just before midnight, was tossed into the sea, a survivable seventy degrees near the equator.

As the ship sank, detritus floated off the deck, and Josh grabbed two wooden deckchairs bearing the name of the vessel. He hung on, circling in the bubbling sea where the ship had floated moments before.

Using both chairs proved difficult to maneuver, and unnecessary. Josh pulled himself aboard a single chair, tied himself on with his belt, and floated with relative ease. He was still floating when the sun came up.

Being an observant master of the stars, he knew he was drifting in a south-southwesterly direction. He was certain there wasn't much out there for over a thousand miles in this section of the Pacific. I'll be long dead of thirst before I reach land.

However, Josh was in error as his deck chair washed him ashore in the dark, three days later. Exhausted, dehydrated, and badly cramping, he cast off the chair, crawled above the high-tide line of seaweed, and collapsed into the sand.

Awaking on the morning of the 24th, by his watch, Josh realized he was in serious need of liquids and nourishment. Fortunately, the beach line teemed with coconut palms, and he was able to smash two of the pods together, get a cupful of liquid, then gnaw on hunks of moist meat. He felt refreshed and energized and, consequently, wondered where he had washed up. Certainly, it was an island somewhere between Hawaii and Australia. Whether it was inhabited or even habitable, he intended to find out.

Ever practical, Dr. Rowbotham accomplished several tasks in what he viewed as the required order. He first built a lean-to from palm fronds and several larger pieces of driftwood. He layered on the fronds to provide cover from both the sun and rain.

He stationed cracked sections of coconuts under the eaves to catch any rain run-off for later consumption. He gathered a few dozen coconuts, as well as some papayas and mangoes from the tree line, and placed his food supply inside his new home. He fashioned a club from a hefty chunk of driftwood, then set off to explore his island.

Josh worked in ever-increasing circles, first up and down his nearby beach, then into the jungle-like cover during the heat of the sun. He heard birds caw at him and smaller animals rushing about in the bush, but he never got close enough to strike at anything.

As Josh explored further afield, he found nothing of note until on November 2nd, several miles down the beach from his camp, where he observed a set of footprints emerging from the jungle and traversing along the beach away from his camp. He placed his foot inside the footprint; it was larger than his own. As the sun was beginning to set, he returned to his encampment with a plan to get started early the next day.

The next morning found him at the trail on the beach by ten o'clock. He retraced the parallel tracks he and the stranger had separately made, then went on, with just the stranger's footprints to guide him.

Following the footprints in the sand, Josh could see the sky was darkening ahead and wondered if the island was due for a tropical storm. He rounded the point and came to an abrupt halt, just like the footprints beneath him.

Where the footprints ended, so did the island. The sky in front darkened and merged into the blackness of space. The sea ended its horizontal position, tumbling over the edge into an empty abyss.

Josh had no idea how to proceed. He sat down on the warm sand, his feet dangling into the nothingness of deep space. Looking over his shoulder, he saw the flat disc of Earth as far as he could see. The breeze faded, leaving the only the sound of the sea thundering over the rim of the Earth.

Professor Josh Rowbotham, resting at the border of earth and space, contemplated issues regarding his survival in this new realm, as well as his choice of a career over forty years ago. If nothing else, he would definitely need to rework his presentation's opening.

Bob Ellis a retired financial services exec and consultant, has lived on three continents and swum in all the oceans!

The Every Beast

Every Friday evening, Terrance and his wife Nancy would catch up with their friends Victor and Hector at a bar in the Florida countryside. Normally, the conversation revolved around sports, politics, or their most recent hunt, but this meetup was different.

"Have you guys heard about the Every Beast?" Hector asked, taking a sip of beer.

Terrance raised his eyebrows out of intrigue. "Every Beast? What's that?"

"Oh, just some rumor," Victor scoffed. "There's been multiple sightings of all kinds of creatures in the forest near here. Just your usual fare: deer, gators, coyotes. Nothing special. But some people are getting the ridiculous idea that it's all the same creature, like some kind of shapeshifter."

"It's more than just a rumor, Vic," said Hector. "My brother says he was out huntin' stag during a full moon, and saw it change with his own eyes!"

"I think he's let those monster movies get to his head."

"It ain't just him, Vic. He asked around, and it turns out that everyone else who had seen it said it was during a full moon, too!"

Victor shot Hector a doubtful look. "Oh, really? And why on a full moon, of all times?"

"Actually, my brother has a theory about that. He says that the full moon must be making the beast change uncontrollably."

Victor shook his head. "Still sounds like mere superstition to me."

Terrance glanced outside the window. The sun was beginning to set. "Isn't there a full moon tonight?" he asked.

"Sure is," Hector replied. "That's what reminded me of it."

Terrance finished his glass of beer and stood up. "Well fellas, you've got me curious. What say we see for ourselves how true this rumor is?"

"I'd love to," said Hector, "but the missus is workin' tonight and I've got to put the kids to bed."

Victor rolled his eyes. "I'd rather not waste my time."

Terrance turned to Nancy, who had been listening to the conversation with a baffled look on her face. "How about you come with me tonight?"

he asked. "I'll need the company."

"Are you sure about this, hun?"

"C'mon, we've hunted together a few times in the past, right? Wasn't it fun?"

Nancy sighed, then looked to Terrance with a tender smile. "Alright, then. If you're so keen on going out there, I might as well be there to keep you out of trouble."

***

Night had fallen. Terrance and Nancy stood in the forest assessing their equipment.

"You look pretty good in camouflage," Terrance commented with a wink.

"You don't look so bad yourself. Did you find everything you needed?"

"Yep. Got my goggles, walkie-talkies, and the rifles." Terrance pulled out a small, half-empty box of rifle rounds.

Nancy glanced at the ammunition. "Is that all?"

"I couldn't find the rest for the life of me! I must've misplaced it somewhere…"

"I'm scared, hun. Are you sure you want to do this?"

"It'll be fine, sweetie. I wanna know what's out here. Besides, it's probably just some ordinary game." Terrance loaded the two rifles and handed one to his wife, as well as a walkie-talkie and a pair of night vision goggles. "Let's split up so we can cover as much ground as possible. If you see it, take the shot. Call me if you need help."

***

As the full moon towered overhead, Terrance crept through the dark forest, scanning the environment for movement with his night vision goggles. Suddenly, he heard a familiar scream nearby.

He pulled out his walkie-talkie in a panic. "Nancy! Are you okay?"

There was no response.

Terrance put the walkie-talkie away and cupped his hands around his mouth. "Nancy, can you hear me?" he called out into the forest.

Again, no response.

Terrance ran in the direction where the scream originated. Once he arrived, he frantically searched the area. The dirt had been shifted, showing signs of struggle. All that was left were night vision goggles and a walkie talkie, next to Nancy's hunting rifle. Not a single round was fired. Terrance collected the ammo from Nancy's rifle, intent on sinking every bullet into the beast that took his wife. He heard growling and a twig snapping shortly after, and boldly crept towards it.

Terrance had arrived at the beast's last location, with a broken twig laying on the ground. There was no animal in sight. However, he did find what appeared to be ordinary gator prints. Knowing that this could be the Every Beast, he followed the trail.

As the trail stretched onward, the beast's stride became longer. Each print became rounded and hoofed. Terrance was no longer following gator prints, but rather the hoofprints of a deer. He continued to follow the trail as it zipped around the trees. Soon after, the prints shifted to wolf-like pawprints. Not long after that, the beast must have changed again, as the spaces between the prints shortened until they merged into one line that slithered deeper into the forest.

Eventually, the trail had stopped. Scanning his surroundings, Terrance caught movement amongst the bushes. It was a mouse, who looked back to Terrance before scurrying away.

"Oh, just a mouse," said Terrance, briefly forgetting the special quirk of this supposed creature. "...Wait a minute!"

He shook his head and ran in the direction towards the mouse.

Without any noticeable tracks to follow, Terrance grew weary, worried that he had lost the creature's trail. Fortunately, he found bear tracks that began seemingly out of nowhere. He followed the tracks until he reached the entrance of a cave. The creature must have changed just before entering the cave, as the last few prints were different. They were bare footprints of a human. Terrance steeled himself and raised his rifle before entering the cave.

As Terrance turned the corner, he found a figure shielding its face. The figure had reached a dead end, with nowhere else to go. Terrance glanced at the figure's clothes which were torn and stretched. The forest camouflage it wore against the cavern walls only made it stand out more. Terrance trembled as the figure slowly uncovered its face.

"Honey," Nancy said timidly, "be a dear and put the gun down."

 **Michael Farrell** was drawn into the world of writing by his childhood dreams and the desire to bring his stories to life. He is a black belt in tae kwon do and has practiced the art for ten years. He also has a background in tumbling.

The Return of a Minor Goddess

Only one person would wear heels to a cemetery in January—the last person I wanted to see. Her footprints in the snow gave her away.

We were once orphans together. We communicated like old married couples—finishing each other's sentences and being comfortable in silence for hours. I knew her better than I knew myself.

"Oh, June." I sat in the car with the heat on. Although eight degrees in Albany, New York isn't unique for January, it's still no fun.

I wore jeans and boots and a heavy winter jacket she said made me look like Grimace from the old McDonalds commercials. It wasn't said in jest.

She'd said it just after the breast cancer took our Aunt Erin. It had been four years from her diagnosis until I took her to the Hospice that Thursday afternoon. By Sunday, she was gone.

"I wish my Juney were here," she'd said on that final ride.

I'd wanted to cry about it all. Our destination. That she pined for the girl who tossed us aside for a bigger life. But I had to be strong. My big sister wasn't there anymore.

"I know." I kept my anger as my own secret.

I could understand if June had left for love. But her Juney left to get away from where she came from, what she was. To get away from us. First in the family to attend college. Then a masters, a doctorate. Publication. She didn't have time for the girl in the Grimace jacket.

After they'd optioned one of her books, she shuttled between from LA to Boston. Not getting here until four days after Aunt Erin died—spending just the afternoon. While I grieved, she talked about the parties, the actress in the adaption of her book. Her commitment to justice.

To me, justice means going to prison for committing a crime. She said it's not that simple. I said it's not that hard. That's when I told her she shouldn't have come. We haven't spoken since.

"Shit."

I try not to curse any more. I'd heard my daughter curse the other day, when the people in the next apartment changed the password on their internet. She had to go to McDonalds to finish her homework.

If I did better, she wouldn't have to curse.

I got out, pulled my hat down and put up my collar. I had to be to work in an hour. Then the other job after that. Bills don't pay themselves, 'specially after Christmas.

The wind bit my face.

Aunt Erin used to take us cross-country skiing, a place where they sold Christmas trees. It didn't matter how cold it was, we'd work up a sweat, then sit by the fireplace in the lodge and drink chocolate. One of the owners liked Aunt Erin, so we skied free, got a Christmas tree, and lots of whipped cream on our chocolate. June let me steal some of hers.

Back home we'd have popcorn for dinner and fall asleep in the living room in our princess sleeping bags. If the movie was scary, June would let me sleep right up next to her. Sometimes I pretended to be scared when I wasn't. I think she knew.

I blinked back a tear. Too cold for crying.

I followed the footsteps, turned the hedge corner just in time to see June put flowers on the grave—long-stem yellow roses. Aunt Erin's favorites. I can't afford flowers.

She stood up, adjusted her mask. You can't catch the Covid alone in a cemetery. That's June, always making a statement.

She wore a fleece-lined denim jacket and baggy jeans. And boots with heels. Had to look good to visit a grave. She hugged herself hard against the wind.

I stood in place. It wasn't the place for a fight.

She turned. She always knew when I was there.

"Hey." My voice was flat.

Her hand went to her mouth. "Oh," I think she said. It was hard to tell with the mask on.

June's steps had always been firm and decisive, even when she was wrong. The woman in front of me shuffled. She tucked a cane under her arm, held out the other as if she were reaching for a railing.

I looked back at the steps. She'd shuffled all the way here. It had to take five minutes in the cold, a long time when you're wearing a denim jacket.

When I turned back, she was right in front of me, her hand at her mouth. When she spoke, her voice was thick.

"I hoped…I wanted…you're here. You're really here."

"Hi, June."

She pulled off the glasses and slid them in her pocket. Her eyes should've pierced two holes in me, but they were shiny with tears.

"What's with the cane?" Nice. Lead with the worst possible thing.

She held her eyes shut a second, then opened them. "I…I got sick last fall. Boston. Four months. They thought I would die."

She nodded toward the gravestone I'd picked. "She was there. I had dreams…she was…she said I had to stop on the way home."

"Back to LA?"

She nodded. "Bradley died. I have to…we both got it. Covid. I'm going home to plan the memorial service."

My breath caught and my hand went to my mouth. He was her husband, a man who saw me as more than June's alcoholic sister who shops at Walmart.

"She…uhh…she told me. In my dream."

"Told you what?"

I winced. My tone sounded like an accusation.

She closed her eyes and more tears came. "That you would come. I'd stop here and you'd come."

"Here I am." I sounded like a…like a bad person.

"I know." Her voice was a whisper now, taken by the wind. Somehow I heard it. "If I said…"

"If you said what?"

"I'm sorry," she said. "So sorry."

It's hard when a god, even a tiny one, says you settled and deserve what you have. No one wants to be rejected by a god. And now, here she was, apologizing.

"I was wrong. So wrong."

No one wants to see their god crumble in front of them.

We stood like that for a time. Me in my Grimace jacket. Her in her fleece denim jacket, holding her cane, hugging herself against the cold.

"I like your jacket." Her eyes almost reached mine as she said it.

I laughed, though I didn't want to. "Takes a special kind of stupid to wear a denim jacket in January."

She laughed back, and whatever bound my heart loosened a little. "It was October. That's what I had."

"I missed you." The wind stung against cheeks I didn't realize were wet.

"Can you forgive me?"

Funny thing is, I cut her off. Told her if she couldn't be proud of me, I didn't want her. I was in the bottle then. June left. Erin suffered. I came apart.

I wanted to say yes, but the bottom part of my face quaked. No words came. The wind couldn't take the wail that released my heart and drove me into my older sister's arms.

Chris Hamilton lives with his wife and angry cat in Lutz, Florida. He wants to know if you'd like a cat.

Queen Ann and the Dragon

"I don't like being cold," said Kimmy.

Ann looked up from the medical equipment she had just finished sterilizing. Streaks of summer light framed the seven-year-old in the doorway, making her look more shadow than human.

Kimmy took a step, her shoes squelching on the clean linoleum. Head to toe, she was dripping mud.

"Stop." Ann held out her hand, freezing Kimmy in place before bursting into laughter. She grabbed a towel and rushed over. Ann wiped mud from her daughter's face, revealing pink, dimpled cheeks.

"What did…" Ann's words trailed off as her eyes adjusted to the sunlight. Her laughter ceased.

Two water hoses blasted water into a growing stream that appeared to have been carved intentionally.

Remain calm, hear her out.

"It's a moat to keep out The Dragon." Kimmy stood tall, hands on hips, feet wide.

"Dragon?"

Kimmy gave a toothy grin. "Yes, my Queen," she said, curtsying mud and grace. "We are safe."

Ann surveyed the damage until her eyes focused across the street. Although she couldn't hear Mrs. Thompson's disapproval, she could feel it. The woman's fiery stare cut the distance. Ann waved. Mrs. Thompson turned and stomped into her home. Ann imagined the click of dragon claws with each step the woman took.

She turned back to Kimmy. "Let's get you cleaned up," she said, wiping another glob of mud from her daughter's nose.

Her watch warned she had fifteen minutes. Fifteen precious minutes before Kevin, Kim's twin, needed his medicine.

Ann considered calling out to Mrs. Thompson for help, but she knew Kim would be collateral damage if she did. The older woman rarely approved of Kimmy's creative adventures, especially when she was pulled into them.

"Turn off that hose," Ann pointed to the one that required a trek through puddles to retrieve, "and meet me in the driveway."

"I'm cold."

"Do it." A small tap on her mud-covered butt spurred the Princess to action.

Ann chose each step carefully, avoiding as much mud as possible. She picked up the second hose in the driveway, crimped it, and waited.

Kicking up mud from every puddle, Kimmy splashed her way to the other hose bib. The stream finally stopped and she hopscotched from puddle to puddle before landing in the moat.

"Kimberly, please."

Kimmy froze, eyes wide, and mouthed "Dragon."

Ann snapped around, losing her grip on the clenched hose.

Mrs. Thompson's "please explain—" was interrupted by the full force of pent-up water.

Ann's hands shot to her mouth to cover both horror and laughter. The hose snaked its way across the driveway, soaking Ann and The Dragon.

Ann chased the hose as Mrs. Thompson turned. The click of claws replaced by the squish of sneakers. Steaming footprints were the only sign she had been there at all.

Ann checked her watch and urged her daughter to hurry. Wide-eyed and giggling, Kimmy obliged, splashing as much mud as possible along the way. They both shivered as the hose washed mud from skin and clothes before making their way back inside.

"Shower." Ann closed the door behind them. "And leave your clothes in the tub."

"I'm cold and I don't like showers."

"The Queen commands." Ann pointed toward the bathroom.

Kimmy curtsied and ran down the hall, leaving a trail of puddling footprints.

A light tap on the wall reminded Ann that Kevin's meds and lunch were overdue. He was hungry and she was late.

She slipped out of her shoes and wet clothes leaving them by the door and rushed down the hall, dodging puddles in bare feet. From the hamper in her room, she grabbed sweatpants and a tank top. They clung to her damp skin as she pulled them on.

She heard Kevin bang on the wall and hurried to the kitchen to fill syringes with his mid-day meds and liquid lunch.

Supplies in hand Ann pushed his door open with her foot. "I'm here." She set the syringes down and stroked her son's hair. Kevin grabbed hold of her wrist. Moving her other hand to coax his fingers to release she asked, "Are you hungry?"

He responded with a smile as he reached a hand through the slots of his hospital bed and pinched her thigh. Her chest warmed and her shoulders relaxed, at the familiar gesture.

She lifted his damp shirt. "Baby, what happened?"

During his nap, he'd pulled his G-button, feeding tube out. Not again. This was the second time this week, and she hadn't replaced the backup. She felt her shoulders instantly tense back up.

"Princess! Our Knight needs us!" Ann heard the shower stop as she tried to return the G-button to Kevin's stomach, but it had been out too long. A distracted Kevin pulled her hair while she worked. In a fluid motion, she grabbed medical tape and secured the G-button into place, a temporary fix.

A missed dose would mean more seizures. Ann squeezed Kevin's cheeks before he could clamp his teeth shut. I'm sorry, I hate this too. With years of practice, she squirted each tube of medication down his throat, holding his mouth shut, waiting for the swallow.

"Ready, mom." Streaks of mud trailed the back of Princess Kimmy's neck as she stood in the doorway, hair pulled into a wet ponytail, wearing pink pants and an orange Halloween shirt, holding Kevin's hospital bag.

"Lead the way." Ann smiled as Kimmy turned towards the front door.

Ann scooped Kevin up and his hands locked in her hair. He laughed as she struggled down the hallway, trying not to slip while carrying her precious Knight.

"Is his wheelchair in the van?" Kimmy held the front door and pressed the key fob to open Kevin's side of the van as Ann squeezed by.

Ann struggled to talk and walk. "Yeah… never took… out last night." Kevin had a good ten pounds on his twin sister.

As she strapped him into his seat, he reached up pulling her face in close. He kissed her big, engulfing her mouth and nose in a sweet sticky mess. When he pulled away his laugh was infectious.

"Ready," Kimmy said, buckling into the seat beside her brother.

"Baby," said Kevin, his one word for everything.

Ann took her place in the driver's seat and began to back out of the driveway, realizing she never turned the second hose off. At the same time, Mrs. Thompson reemerged in flip-flops.

Ann stopped and waved The Dragon closer. "I'm headed to the hospital. Can you turn off the water and lock the front door?"

"Of course."

Ann watched in the rearview mirror as Kimmy's dragon, Mrs. Thompson, made her way to the hose. She knew from past experience when she returned home, the muddy footprints and wet clothes would be washed, and a casserole would be waiting in the fridge.

"Oh no!" Ann braked again. "I forgot shoes."

"I remembered." Kimmy tossed the muddy pair of sneakers Ann had left by the front door onto the passenger seat.

Ann smiled back through the rearview mirror. A Princess, a Knight, and a friendly Dragon. She wondered how she ever got so lucky.

Hope N. Griffin lives in Brandon, FL, with her partner, children, rescue pets, and neglected houseplants. She is a published author and freelance writer. To learn more about Hope and her writing, visit www.HopeNGriffin.com.

Sands of Time

"Dad, we feel, John and I, that you would be so much more comfortable in Sandy Acres," my fifty-year-old daughter Jeanne tells me.

The name alone indicated the transient nature of the 'home' for the ageing. Sand, at the mercy of wind and water.

"I am fine," I say.

My retirement money pays for the livelihood of others. My twice-a-week housekeeper cleans the rooms that once bustled with life. They are now merely historic mementoes. My jack-of-all-trades cares for the garden, his efforts shrunk to trimming hedges. He does other things too. I'm not sure what. Perhaps I should ask Jeanne. The lawn service maintains the life of the grass, sustaining it for a fee, with water and fertilizer. Beds of roses and perennials have gradually yielded to St Augustine grass—so much easier to take care of.

Jeanne insisted on a service to deliver ready-prepared meals daily. My daughter, bless her heart, is convinced I cannot prepare my own food. I admit to an intention tremor, which translates to clumsiness which sometimes causes me to drop things. Nothing serious, except perhaps the kitchen knife that speared my foot. Of little consequence. The bleeding really didn't warrant the emergency room.

Who can understand the profound need to hold on to the pattern of life developed over years, until they face the inevitability of their own mortality?

My mind screams at me as it separates gradually from my body, taking with it memories, of the marks I have left on life. This decline is my secret. I cannot share the fears with Jeanne. It would strengthen her argument to sentence me to confinement. Confinement, isolation from all that is familiar. This is my biggest fear.

Is this true, or is it my imagination, driven into overdrive as it becomes harder and harder to retain awareness of the present? I make a note of my feelings.

Thank goodness for the monitor and keyboard. They provide an immediate record of recent thought, which is yet vulnerable to the whim of the delete key. While it exists, while I can still recognize the imprint of black and white on the screen, it is my increasingly tenuous hold on reality.

77

Footprints

My memories of life are like footprints in the sand, gradually washed away as the inexorable rise of the tide bathes it in its ever-increasing depth. I can still remember the photograph of the footprints of a mother and child, Afarensis, I recall, made almost three million years ago. Preserved in wet volcanic ash, never washed away. One of our earliest ancestors. Who can claim to leave such a mark on history?

All systems have a natural lifespan.

Jeanne, my baby, who I remember with shock is now in her fifties, tells me, with a smile, that forgetfulness is natural as one ages. This reminds me that my journey is nearing its end. Jeanne and John have yet a good part of their journey to travel before they face whether they have left an imprint on history.

The tragedy is that recent memories will be the first to hesitate on the edge of remembrance, to fade and disappear, gradually at first then with increasing speed, much as the sense of time accelerates from infancy to maturity. Eventually, my memories of Jeanne will be of a small helpless infant that I could hold in my cupped palms. I cannot admit this to her. Not yet. Although I am aware that by the time it is safe to tell her, the reason, a recent thought, might well be lost.

Jeanne is worried because I sometimes forget the name of the grocery store, or the items I need. Names have always posed a problem of recall for me. But this day-to-day living stuff is of little concern. I had the sense to arrange automatic payment for deliveries. I know I can recall things eventually. It sometimes takes a little time and then I can write them on the screen. I used checks before my tremor obliterated my signature. I bought a wireless keyboard with larger keys to reduce the chances for trembling fingers to hit more than one key at a time.

I take pride in my vocabulary. I learned most of it at a young age and have the satisfaction of knowing that it will last much longer than recent memories. I still subscribe to a science digest. The papers keep me abreast of the progress in a field I once reveled in. Although, I must admit, I sometimes have to read them two or three times. Luckily, I can save them, so the memory is preserved.

Sandy Acres, Sandy Acres. I keep repeating it because I know this is a recent memory and in danger of being forgotten. I have a pact with myself that when it disappears and I cannot remember where I am going, that will be the time. A moment. Time for what? What was my train of thought? Will I have forgotten my decision?

I record my thoughts in a personal file. Jeanne knows I am writing things down. She doesn't know what, and I think she is a little scared. I have not told her the password. That will be an obstacle on her path. We all have them. Why should she be spared?

Footprints

The memories of her mother will be the most painful to forget. My rational self, while it still exists, wonders if I will remember that I have forgotten? But they extend far back in time. They are part of the safe place that I can retire to. The private place that no-one else shares.

***

A few days later, I think, I'm not sure, perhaps it was weeks, I am still aware of pieces of time, someone awoke me from a nap.

"Dad," I hear someone call.

I don't understand. As I fumble to remember, I recognize the face of my daughter. We retreat together into my mind, awakening a present where I once lived. A safe place.

I remember. "You're Jeanne." I smile.

She holds me around the knees, peering up at my face. "Can we run in the sand, Daddy?"

Robert Hart , a retired veterinarian, Bob and his novelist wife, Veronica Helen, live in Ormond Beach. Author of many articles and stories, three pet books and a book of short stories, he is a regular contributor to the annual FWA collections.

Tiny Footprints

Allison was tall with a tiny footprint. At least it was small for her height. Everything around her had a tiny footprint, the pink and blue framed pictures of her babies' feet on the antique hue of the ranch house wall. The cabbage patch dolls she made had a little cauliflower footprint.

She wanted a pool in her backyard. She was a California girl, only now she lived in Kentucky. That was okay. The pool could be heated and usable from April through October—as long as it didn't snow.

Footprints were a trademark of snow: dog prints, round and well-spaced; squirrel prints with slews; deer prints in the country, and rabbit prints yards and yards apart. They all melded beneath a bright winter sun in the cerulean sky.

"What's so funny?" her husband, Will, asked when the pool first went in.

"I was just picturing bare-footed people prints in the snow around the lip of the pool."

"Are you really planning to swim in the snow?"

"Only in the hot tub," she said skipping a toe-drippy footprint on the hot tub stairs.

Will turned her around and they went in together, soaking and splashing as they made their next vacation plans.

"Let's go to California and see the kids."

"Got to," she said. "It's Lindy's graduation."

That's where she started feeling bad. She didn't know what was wrong exactly, just a cramping inside, and an ominous feeling about it.

She didn't have to leave all her wet footprints beside her own pool. In addition to the Timeshare in California, Allison and Will had a condo in Florida. Down there, they spent most of their days making footprints in the sand, the dry sand that caved in on them, the wet sand that held them till the waves washed them away. Allison strolled the beach in her black and yellow swimsuit, leaving her small footprint and her big smile behind.

Their final trip was the best one. They left dancing footprints in the setting sun, dined in the light of a rising moon.

Allison looked out across the rippling water. Her smile was sad.

"What is it?" Will asked. "You look unhappy."

"On the contrary. I was thinking how great it is to be alive."

They went for a late swim after dinner and washed the salt water off before bed. Allison stepped out of the shower, leaving a soggy footprint on the rug she crocheted to keep from slipping on the tile floors. She was always doing something, except lately; she hadn't felt like doing much of anything. Something was definitely wrong, but she didn't want to know.

Her footprints became uneven because of her limping. When Will asked what was wrong she said her stomach hurt.

"So, you're limping?"

"Well, it's not my stomach. It's my abdomen. It catches when I walk."

He helped her into the car for the trip home and kept watch from the corner of his eye as she listlessly stitched a quilt by hand while they traveled.

They got home on Saturday night, and Sunday, like every Sunday, they went to church. They entered the choir loft, the plush, red carpet smashed down with their footprints as they went to their seats.

Allison sang soprano. Will sang bass. The choir was in the middle of their anthem when his beeper went off. Will dashed out the side door, waving goodbye. He took the car. Friends drove Allison home.

She was feeling too puny to go to practice that Wednesday night. On Thursday she made a doctor's appointment. A week later, the doctor called her with the bad news.

"I'm going to sew God a new robe," she told Will when he got in from work.

"What?"

"The Lord is calling me home."

"Allison? What are you saying?"

"I saw the doctor while you were gone. I ..." she sniffed, "I have late stage cancer. There's nothing they can do."

Will sat down suddenly in the closest chair, bending double as if gut-punched. "The doctor told you this—on the phone—while you were home alone?"

"Yes."

"I'll kill the—man."

Allison went and sat on his lap. "It's going to be all right. I'm not afraid. I know where I'm going. And," she said, hopping up, "I have lots of work to do."

The next few months were filled with footsteps to the cancer center for palliative treatments. Then the footsteps ceased. She worked from chairs and eventually her bed. She had the boy's baby blanket to crochet. The girl's was finished. Two quilts weren't done.

The minister's wife, left-handed like Allison, finished crocheting the baby blanket. Will's sister did the quilts. Allison's family had come and gone. Her church family was there when she left her pool and her condo, and her beautiful works behind—and a very large footprint on Will's heart.

Bonnie B. Herrick was published in the FWA 2016 Collection, in the FWA magazine and the Kentucky Literary Magazine. She has been a finalist and semi-finalist for the RPLA awards.

Footprints

Two of the biggest footprints Toby had ever seen were right there on the muddy riverbank. The rain had stopped, and the prints were beginning to harden. He had almost stepped on them, but he drew back and gaped at what he saw.

Other footprints, fainter and less distinct, led away into the trees. Animal prints were also scattered around. But that massive set of footprints caused the back of Toby's neck to tingle, and the few hairs on his young arms to stand on end. He was twelve and small for his age. He shuddered to imagine how tall and powerful this creature must be.

The prints were easily eighteen inches long, with the imprint of some kind of soft covering, like a bootie or moccasin. This could not be an animal. Only humans would make their own shoes.

Toby tore himself away from the fearsome footprints and continued up the side of the mountain. He'd been headed for his secret place, high above his father's farm. He rarely slipped away on a workday, but today's toil and drudgery were more than he could bear. His father was ill-tempered, the other workers rough and bitter, and all of them were on edge from low food rations. Life for him felt stern and hard.

***

Months earlier, Toby had discovered the small cave entrance covered by thorn bushes. He'd been stalking a rabbit when it slipped through those bushes and vanished. He had peered through the bushes and discovered a small, clear pathway behind them where he could maneuver on his belly along the face of the rock. He wouldn't have risked the sharp thorns if he hadn't seen the opening in the rock.

He had slithered and crawled inside the cave and sat up in the soft sand. It had enough room to lie down and stretch out, a perfect place to be alone and think his own thoughts. It would be a warm place when cold winds blew, and a dry place when the rain fell. Best of all, it would be a secret all his own.

***

Now he hurried there, hoping nothing watched and discovered his hiding place. He jumped at every sound of rustling leaves or snapping twigs. Even if he had a weapon, he'd stand no chance against a hungry wolf or mountain lion—or a giant. He'd heard of giants in faraway lands, but he'd always assumed they were like fairy tales, stories to entertain while sitting at campfires in the evening. Now giants seemed like a horrifying possibility.

Would his father ever believe him? He might think his boy had seen the footprints of a grizzly bear. But Toby knew the difference between a man's footprint and the wide paw print of a bear.

He found his familiar trail and climbed higher up the hillside. When he reached the thorn bushes, he stood behind a tall oak tree and peeked around, turning in all directions. There were too many places for cover; he couldn't be sure he wasn't being observed. Weariness made him surrender his caution and scuttle along behind the bushes to the shelter of his cave.

Toby knew his pa would be worried and angry by now, but he curled up on the soft white sand and fell asleep. He dreamed of bounding rabbits and yapping dogs. He dreamed of swimming in the creek on a hot summer day. And he awoke to discover the sun was setting.

He must hurry while there was still light enough to find his way back home. He crawled out of the cave and inched along behind the bushes. He grew still as a stone when he saw the ground ahead of him, in the fading light.

Two giant feet, bound in buckskin, awaited him. He was too frightened to move, but he heard the words, "Come out." The voice blew at him like a strong wind. Toby hesitated, but he knew the thorn bushes would not protect him. And his curiosity was now almost as great as his fear.

He crawled a little farther, then rose to his feet and stared upward into the face of the powerful man towering over him. At home, the barn door was tall enough for a work horse to walk through. This man would have to duck at that same door.

The giant was hairless with bluish gray skin. He wore a short robe of bearskin and he carried no weapon that Toby could see.

The language Toby heard was unfamiliar to him, but he could feel its meaning. In the now silent air, more words filled his mind.

"Why are you here alone?"

"It's my place, my secret place. I'm happy here," Toby answered.

The hulking figure studied him, then sent more words into his mind. "If you are hungry, cold, naked, afraid for your life . . . where will you go?"

Toby watched the giant's mouth move, speaking foreign words. Still, he understood the question. He dropped his head and answered, "I will go to my father." Toby did not move or lift his eyes. He waited for another question, but none came.

His eyes darted to the huge feet, but he saw only footprints. Startled, he turned wildly in every direction, listening for the sound of crashing underbrush, and watching to catch a glimpse of the giant. The bluish man had vanished.

Toby was drawn to the footprints and he stepped into the heel sections. His small feet only took up a third of the space.

His mind went back to a game he played at home, walking barefoot early in the morning, following the footprints of his father's boots, and hopping from one print to another, unable to match his father's stride.

His pa was strict with lots of rules. Time and again, he'd told Toby he must learn to work like a man if he wanted to survive in this world. Mostly, Toby just wanted to play and have fun, throw a stick for the farm dog, or hunt for crawdads in the creek.

But he knew who kept him safe at night, who told him tall tales by the kitchen fireplace, and who took care of him when he had a stomach ache or a skinned knee. Toby was just a little boy, but having faced a giant, he felt more like a man. And he appreciated his father with a newfound maturity. Yes, he'd get a lecture when he got home. But he'd be with his father again, and he'd be proud to follow in Pa's footsteps.

Toby found himself running full speed down the hillside toward home, racing to beat the darkness. He was not concerned with any giant lurking nearby. The soft breeze whispered his name, and the cicadas sang to him as he ran to the safe arms of his father.

Ellen Holder, originally from North Carolina, is a happy resident of Central Florida. She and her husband are entertainers. She enjoys reading, dancing, and gardening, but finds time for writing at all hours of the day or night.

A Perfect Size Six

I nudge you awake. "John, do you hear that?"

"Hear what?" you grumble through a fog of sleep.

"Footsteps…"

You roll over and face me. "Not again…go back to sleep."

I shut my eyes, but sleep never comes while she walks around our house. She's always with us—between the sheets and pillows. She's there when you press your body against mine.

***

In 1974, Amalia and I were roommates in Alphabet City while we studied at NYU. Both of us English majors. Both of us hanging out in the Slaughtered Lamb with notepads in hand—hoping J.D. Salinger or Ferlinghetti would walk in at any moment and notice us. We fantasized we'd chirp, "we're writers." Then the novelist and poet, respectively, would grab our writing, read our prose and verses, shout their praise of our genius, and we'd be published in next Sunday's *New York Times Magazine*.

Instead you walked in—a dead ringer for James Dean if he'd lived past his twenties—exactly my type. A Marlboro dangling from your lower lip, the suede elbow patches on your tweed jacket worn and tattered.

The Lamb was packed with coeds that night, and there was nowhere to sit, except next to Amalia and me. She in a white linen, Givenchy dress and perfect size-six, red, YSL pumps—I in a cotton frock I'd owned since high school and a pair of size-eight earth shoes.

"May I?" you asked when you came up to our table.

Amalia scooted over to give you the edge of our bench and fluttered her false eyelashes.

I sipped my drink and let the sloe gin fizz tickle my nose, knowing full well that was as much of a thrill I'd get that evening.

"You girls come here often?"

My brain screamed, CLICHÉ PICK-UP LINE, but my lips didn't move.

Amalia nodded and shot you a full-toothed, bright-white, school-girl grin—a smile that could get any man to fall into bed with her.

"What do you girls do?"

"We're writers," the two of us answered nearly in unison.

"I am too," you said. "I write for a psychiatric journal."

And that was all Amalia needed to hear to swoon into your arms. She swooned with you on our walk back to Alphabet City. The two of you swooned so long, I had to sleep on a bench outside our building that night—bunk beds aren't made for three, especially in 400 square feet of space.

Two weeks later, Amalia moved in with you, and I was left to pay the rent on my meager freelance editor's salary. The Sunday after my eviction notice arrived, I spotted Amalia smiling out from a page in the *Times* "Styles" section. The caption read, "Dr. and Mrs. John Salazar of Scarsdale, NY. Married, April 26, 1974." Amalia's finally made it into *The New York Times*, I thought.

In June I moved out of my Manhattan apartment back to my parents' modest Hartsdale home—just across the Bronx River from the Scarsdale office of Dr. Salazar.

Out of work and nearly out of my mind trapped in the house where I grew up, I started taking long walks. Walks that gave me time to think and plan with every step. It was on a warm July day that I passed a grand, old house on a quiet Scarsdale street. Annexed at its side was an office with a sign that read Dr. J. Salazar, Psychiatrist.

I paced the block a few times to build up courage to visit my ex-roommate. I went to the front of the house, climbed the stone steps to the huge front door, and rang the bell. Amalia answered perfectly coiffed and impeccably dressed. She wrapped me in her arms. "Oh, I never thought I'd see you again. Come in…come in. I think I got some good news in the mail today."

Her invitation was an opportunity I'd never expected on my first visit.
***

The obits in the following weekend's *Times* described Amalia's death as "a tragic accident, in which the newlywed tumbled down a flight of stairs and fell on a letter opener that pierced her heart."

If only Amalia hadn't lost her footing as she read me her acceptance letter to *The Sunday Times Magazine*.

Although the service was a stone's throw from my parents' house, I decided not to attend Amalia's funeral. Instead I waited two weeks and called you to extend my condolences.

I had to jog your memory until you recalled our meeting in the Slaughtered Lamb, but once you did, you invited me to visit your office for counseling, comforting, and a cup of tea.

By our third meeting, the teacups were filled with Jack Daniels, and we were more than "comforting" each other on your couch.

Two weeks later you asked me to marry you—widowers in mourning are always easy prey, even for homely girls like me.

The next day we dashed to the Westchester County Clerk's office and tied the knot. The ring you slipped on my finger closed the circle of what I'd hoped for all along.

A month after we married, I moved Amalia's urn from your bedroom to the attic. In the half-light of the upstairs space, I polished and rubbed its brass as if it were Aladdin's lamp—perhaps wishing Amalia would disappear. "Rest well, friend," I said, set her on a shelf, and trudged down the steps.

***

While I sit reading in the living room, I hear you tapping on your typewriter in the annex. When the clicking stops, and the light under your office door fades from yellow to black. I listen for your footsteps up the stairs to the master bedroom.

Once the bedroom door creaks shut, I put down my book, tiptoe into your office, and rifle through your desk. In the top drawer I find a draft of an article you're writing for The American Journal of Psychiatry. I can't understand the technical language, but you're using me as a test subject for a drug called physostigmine—the red pill you tell me is a vitamin. You note it has little effect on my nightly panic attacks. You write about how I shake you awake and ask you to listen for footsteps in the house. Footsteps that torment me, but you sleep through.

My eyes open wide when I read your notes in the margin:

My wife's delirium may be schizoid paranoia. She says she feels my late wife between us when we make love. Since she moved my late wife's urn to the attic, she tells me she hears footsteps...

Then I hear them...lumbering down the attic stairs, padding across the living room, shuffling at the threshold of the office. I fling open the door. There's no one there, but across the deep, shag-pile of the living room carpet I make out a trail of perfect size-six footprints.

Paul Iasevoli has had short stories and poems published in various national journals. He has won several RPLA awards and his work has appeared in the FWA Collection over the years. He's author of the award nominated novella, *Winter Blossoms*, published by Beaten Track Publishing. *pauliasevoliwords.com*

Footprints Must Bring Change

He was used to discrimination. For 46 years, it had been a way of life for him, his family, his friends, and the whole side of town where he lived. When his daughter was born, he was grateful she was a girl. There was no need for more black men in this world. There was too much aggression, too much anger, and too much prejudice. Too many footprints that led to nowhere positive and nothing good.

He was human, and he erred. He drank, maybe too much. He tried to pass a counterfeit $20 bill. But his biggest crime was simply being black. The last time in his life the police were called because of his actions was that counterfeit bill. They handcuffed him. He pleaded not to be put in the back seat of the cruiser because of his claustrophobia. He begged for mercy. He did what the officers told him to do.

They put him on the ground and then put a blue knee on George Floyd's neck. Repeatedly, we hear George saying, "I can't breathe. Please, sir, I can't breathe." He even called for his mother. In the end, it did not matter what he said or how much he begged. After all, he was black.

Did that mean he was less than a man? Less than a human? Less deserving than someone with less pigment? Were his footprints in life less worthy?

Eight minutes and 46 seconds later, George Floyd was dead. Still, the officer knelt on his neck, not moving until ordered to do so by paramedics. Hundreds of years' worth of injustices against thousands of black people were the footprint George Floyd's death engraved in people's hearts around the globe. The entire world took to the streets to say his name, to seek justice, to seek change.

All these footprints must bring real change.

Chrissy Jackson has been a lover of words and books since the age of three, first published at age ten, and writes continuously. A voracious reader, she has no favorite genre or author, preferring only a sunny spot, sounds of waves, and a book in which to lose herself.

Footprints in the Snow

Keeping a normal schedule in Alaska required discipline, something I'd always lacked. On cold January nights, when the sun set before supper and wouldn't properly rise again 'til lunch, I understood why so many animals hibernated. By 7:00 p.m., I'd pulled on my fleece pajamas and fuzzy socks and curled on the sofa in front of the television. I've become my mother.

I turned on the television, already set to a cable news broadcast. "We remind the people of Eagle River and the surrounding areas to remain vigilant as hikers continue to go missing—" I switched to Netflix. My husband's the one who watched the news. Terrible things didn't happen in our quaint town, that's what made it special. I made Dean get us an alarm system and I only left the house during the brief daylight hours. If we weren't safe, who was?

The front door opened, and I heard the familiar rhythm of Dean punching in the security code. He wiped his feet at the door but didn't take off his shoes.

"You're not staying?" I asked, not looking up from the medical drama I'd chosen.

"Sorry, Elisa, can't," he said from the hall. "We're doing night builds all week to get this project finished. I'll be sleeping in my trailer onsite. Just came to grab an overnight."

He worked so hard for us. Ever since getting promoted to foreman, he'd spent days and nights at building sites, sometimes hundreds of miles away. But he always brought me to the unveilings, like little vacations.

"You want me to make you some coffee?" I asked.

"Thanks, but I stopped at a drive-through on my way," he called from the bedroom.

After a moment, I heard his footsteps behind me. I tilted my head back as he leaned down to kiss me goodbye. He smelled terrible. I hoped he didn't track mud on the carpet.

"Love you," I said.

He'd already headed for the door. "Love you, too. Sorry for working so much." The storm door banged shut behind him, and a moment later, I heard his truck pull out of the driveway. I'd be sleeping alone for a few nights, may as well have some wine. I paused my show and went to the kitchen for a glass.

A chill crept over me. I shivered. One would think houses in a place that's cold nine months of the year would be less drafty. I looked around to see the front door ajar. I rolled my eyes as I realized that, in addition to not closing the door all the way, I hadn't heard Dean reactivate the alarm. He must've been running late.

I walked to the alarm to activate the nighttime setting but gagged at the smell of something foul. The welcome mat where Dean wiped his feet was caked in mud and smelled worse than he had. I pushed the storm door out, intending to toss the offensive mat outside, when I saw footprints leading to the door from around the side of the house.

I flicked the outside lights on, illuminating the deep footprints in the bright snow. "Dean?" I called. No, he couldn't be out here. I'd heard his truck leave, and the footprints were clearly walking toward our door, not away from it.

The prints coming from the back of the house looked the same as footprints walking away from the door to the driveway where they met tire tracks. What was Dean doing in the backyard? He kept supplies and tools back there sometimes. Maybe he'd had to drop off something.

I felt a twist in my stomach. Something wasn't adding up. I pulled on my boots and coat and followed the footprints behind the house. I felt a bit silly. I never considered myself a suspicious wife. Dean never gave me a reason to be. He was always so loyal and dedicated.

But the tracks didn't lead to his toolshed, or the woodpile, or even to the tarped fishing boat. The prints trailed into the woods that marked the end of our property. I saw a glint of something in the snow and bent to pick it up, a pink flashlight on a carabiner, the kind campers hook to their backpacks. It wasn't mine. I clicked the button, and a beam of LED light brightened the tree line. The tracks became less defined once they entered the woods, but they could still be followed.

But why follow them? It was late, and people were going missing from these woods. On the other hand, Dean had been working a lot this winter. But he'd worked a lot every winter. And every summer. In fact, he'd said summer was the busy season.

I won't go far.

Using the found flashlight to guide me, I followed the tracks into the woods. The sleeping bushes posed some obstacle, low to the ground and close together, but I found the footprints again.

The cuffs of my pants grew damp as snow clung to them and melted from my body heat. My fingers grew red with cold as I shifted the freezing flashlight from one hand to the other. I should have turned back, but I'd come so far. I needed to know where these tracks led.

I broke out of the brush onto a hiking trail I recognized from the pamphlet we got when our relator sold us the house. I didn't care much for hiking, but Dean did, and he saw having a path a quarter mile from the house as a huge selling point. He spent most of his days off in summer on this path.

The tracks lead down the pathway, lit by two bright headlights from a parked car. I approached the car cautiously, and as I got closer, I recognized it as Dean's company van, still running. Had he left this van here and walked home? I tugged the driver's side door handle, but it was locked, passenger's too. Why hadn't he just told me he'd locked his keys in the ignition?

The footprints, I realized, led from the back of the van. He must've gotten something out the back and closed up, not realizing the front was locked. He was a forgetful man, keys, anniversaries, dates. He'd forget his own head if it weren't on his shoulders. Or maybe he just didn't care.

As I circled around back, something crunched under my foot. A cellphone in a pink glitter case lay on the ground, screen smashed. My flashlight caught a shimmer on the rear door, ice crystals spreading over a red stain. My breath caught in my throat. Had Dean been hurt? I reached for the door, compelled to try every entrance to the running van, and pulled the handle. To my surprise, it opened.

The flashlight's beam landed on its owner's face. Her mouth hung open, still in terror. Her down parka had been ripped to shreds. Her bright red hair matched the red spilling from a gash that ran vertically down her stomach.

In the distance, sirens wailed.

I dropped my light.

Dean wouldn't be back. He left me, shattered, to pick up the pieces.

I needed to hide this.

Rome Johnson & Kaitlin Thern have been writing together since high school and credit the stories they create as the secret to their marriage. The pair currently work for the Tampa Pioneer, where Kaitlin is Senior Editor and Rome is a featured writer. They are available for commissions at *alignable.com/ lithia-fl/ union-writing.*

Charm School

It wasn't a Charm School per se, just six classes at the YWCA, but Nora's skin prickled when a co-worker asked if she wanted to go with her. Before Nora married and moved to the big city, Richmond, Virginia, she'd haunted the newsstand during her work breaks looking at fashion and style magazines. It was an open, corner newsstand in her small Texas town that looked exactly like the ones in the bustling cities she dreamed of. Nora even grew fond of the sound of balls clicking in the pool hall next door. The real lure was seeing in the slick magazines the eloquent results of women who surely went to charm school, who knew how to dress, apply makeup and walk. Nora surmised body position, the pose, and the walk were the real keys to charm and sophistication. She tried in her own way to imitate their "charm." Now she would learn their secrets.

As Gladys maneuvered her car into the parking space, Nora took in the ancient, red-brick building on a downtown side street. A very old desk sat to the side of the entrance and the lady there pointed them upstairs to where classes were held. On the floor above the classrooms a revolving group of women lived, marking time until they got over a crisis or could afford a place of their own, Gladys told her. The YWCA was a place of refuge. The building gave off the scent of old musty wood, perfumes, and furniture oil. They climbed the creaky stairs to the second floor. On their right a door with a small, typed card, "Charm School" beckoned.

Inside the high-ceilinged room heavy, serious, oak chairs formed a semi-circle. Most were filled. A blackboard hung at the front. The wide windows across one end looked out onto the street. The women appeared to span the ages of early twenties to sixties. No one spoke to anyone except those they came with. Nora wasn't in Texas anymore.

The door opened behind them and they all turned as a tall, slim blonde wearing a black sheath with hair in a French roll walked gracefully to the front of the classroom. Her only adornments were simple gold earrings and a small gold watch. She turned her palm up to look at the watch.

"Welcome, ladies." Everyone smiled and nodded. Then Adele introduced herself. She was a model. A real model. And she looked like the ones in Vogue. Maybe not as much makeup, but otherwise… Adele told them six weeks was not enough time to cover all they needed to know, but they would learn how to dress for their own best look, the importance of mild exercise, and a healthful diet, as well as the proper way to sit and walk. Yes, walk. They would start with nutrition. That was a bit of a disappointment. Adele held up a book with a pale teal cover and pink spine that read, Mirror, Mirror On The Wall, authored by Gayelord Hauser.

"This is my Bible," she said, "this and Gayelord Hauser's Look Younger, Live Longer, published a few years ago. This one just came out and I would suggest all of you buy a copy and use it as your guide."

It was fresh off the press in 1961. Nora bought a copy the next week, although a bit skeptical she would learn charm from a book. His passages on walking referred to his clients who loved to walk for exercise, clients like Greta Garbo, Marlene Dietrich and Ingrid Bergman. He advertised himself as guru to the stars. And apparently to Adele. That was good enough for Nora. She was in this class to learn and she wanted to BE Adele. After the second week Nora turned her watch around so she could also gracefully glance at it with upturned wrist. Her hair wasn't quite long enough for a French twist, but she'd grow it.

The next two weeks they discussed more nutrition and table manners, shaking hands, and other etiquette. Meantime, Hauser's book had her lying on a slant board feet up. Her slant board was the same as Greta Garbo's—a propped ironing board.

The fourth week Adele discussed fashion, narrowed down to what fashion was right for them individually. She shared that she called her black sheath her uniform and indeed she wore it every time. It was her basic, she explained, on which she added a jacket, scarf, or jewelry to fit the occasion. The class began to speak up a little more and ask questions. Then Adele asked them to wear the outfit they thought they looked best in to the next class. It could be anything. Casual, dressy, or anything in between. Whatever made them feel most attractive.

"That's easy," Nora told Gladys, "I really do like my black sheath, and it kinda looks like Adele's. I'm going to buy a hat to go with it, though."

Gladys said, "I'll just wear my slacks and a nice sweater. I always feel best in those."

Nora headed to the new store in town. It was called K-Mart, a discount store, something new in the market. As Nora plunged into the hat section she saw a familiar figure. Adele was shopping at a discount store. Nora was sure Adele saw her, but quickly turned away. Right at that moment she spied the hat. It was black, bucket shaped straw with a wide black ribbon around the crown with a large bow. Nora couldn't wait for the next class.

Gladys arrived looking natural and comfortable. Nora's garter belt and hose (seams perfectly straight) were not comfortable, but stylish. Adele nodded at Nora when she stood for inspection.

"Very nice, but perhaps you'd feel even better without the bucket hat that shortens your figure," Adelle said, "and less jewelry."

Nora was ready to go home, get comfortable, and prepare for next week's class.

The last class would be on the proper way to walk, Adele announced.

When they entered Adele stood at the blackboard drawing footprints across the whole board—one footprint in front of the other.

Nora whispered to Gladys, "Finally!"

"I'm glad you're happy. I don't see anything wrong with the way we walk now. We get where we want to go."

Nora shook her head in disbelief.

"I'd like you to stand up, class, and push your chairs back. Now we are going to walk following the footprint chart, one foot in front of the other, derrieres held in."

It was a lot harder than the models made it look. Some snickered, but not Nora. She concentrated on the footprints though her hips hurt.

"Keep your eye on the footprints on the board and don't think about it. Your body will learn to follow your feet smoothly. With practice you'll walk like a model.

"Oops! Someone help Nora up, please. That's it, try again, Nora."

Adele checked the time again. "Darn, I've got to get this watchband tightened," and she turned the watch face to the top of her wrist.

Nora did the same on the way home—and she never practiced the walk again.

Beda Kantarjian short stories have appeared online, Orlando Sentinel, and in three anthologies. She placed second in Bethune Short Story Contest. This is her tenth Collections story, including a Top Ten in 2013. Her creative non-fictions have placed first and second in RPLA. She is co-founder/coordinator of Seminole County Writers.

Footprints in the Dirt

Tom stepped, barefoot, from the darkened house onto the front porch and let the sunlight wash over him. He recalled the days of his youth when he would stand on this porch and enjoy the sun's warmth as it caressed him. And now? He sighed. Well, he had the memories.

Tom rolled the legs of his faded overalls to his calves and stood. Inhaling, he thought he should detect nearby blooming flowers, but the air carried no detectable scent.

"Doesn't matter. It's still a nice day."

Hand hovering above the handrail, he negotiated the two steps down to the flagstone walkway, turned right at the gate, and started for the barn, calling for the dog as he went.

"Jake, let's go, boy. Time for our walk."

He set his eyes on the tree line and the worn path to the creek—their destination.

The breeze stirred the remaining autumn leaves. He lifted his face into the wind. "God, but I've missed this."

He turned and called again, "Jake, c'mon, boy. Squirrel."

From the open barn door burst a black-and-tan hound, all legs and ears, tongue lolling, eyes bright with an expression that looked like pure joy to Tom.

"Good, boy." He bent, snatched a pinecone, and tossed it. Jake retrieved, as usual, dropping it at his feet, waiting for another toss.

Four more times, and they came to the path.

"Look for 'em, Jake," he said, knowing the old dog loved to hunt.

Jake loped along the trail, head down, graying muzzle inches from the ground, tail wagging.

Tom followed and felt a smile lift the corners of his mouth.

Sunlight filtered through the leaves; their thinning numbers allowed dappled light to play on the fresh carpet of gold, red, and yellow.

He remembered, as a child, the feel of cool crisp leaves under his feet. Maple, alder, birch, and pine grew in abundance on his twenty-acre farm, and he always loved partaking in the seasonal change. Walking barefoot among the fallen leaves was a tradition—his anyway. His and Jake's, he amended.

The smile slipped for a moment as he thought of his son, David. "Never enjoyed this like we do, ain't that right, boy?" Jake bounded back, expectant.

He found a stick and threw it far along the path. Jake did what he loved to do, and Tom laughed softly. "We find joy where we can. If we're lucky enough."

Jake barked, and Tom answered, "Comin', don't rush me." He picked up the pace and caught up with the dog at their destination. Jake barked again, his tail slapping his flanks.

The soft gurgle of water over stones beckoned, and he pushed through the thicket and into the small clearing bordering their creek. Jake ambled down the slope, stopping at the edge of the spring-fed rivulet. Tom eased himself to the ground and sighed with contentment.

This place was theirs, their retreat from the daily monotony of farm life. He pulled his knees close, wrapping his arms tight around them, and listened as the forest shared its eternal message: life, death, rebirth, ad infinitum.

Jake returned, laid beside him, and chuffed his example of contentedness.

"Nice day, hey, Jake?"

No answer was necessary or given.

"Yeah, I agree."

The sound of an approaching car disturbed the peace, and he turned to see a familiar sedan pull into the drive at the farmhouse.

"Well, would you look who it is?" He stroked Jake's head. "My boy's comin' to visit."

A young man stepped from the driver's side and held the rear door open. A smaller version of the man hopped to the ground and looked around, eyes wide and curious. A young, pregnant woman emerged from the passenger door and moved to the farmhouse steps, where she sat. She flapped a hand at the two who, after some verbal exchange Tom couldn't hear, set out in his and Jake's direction.

"Are they comin' here?" he asked of Jake.

Jake woofed and returned his muzzle to his paws.

Tom watched as his grandson sprinted toward the barn.

"The hell?" Tom cupped his hands and yelled, "Stay outta the barn, son, the loft is rotting."

The barn door squealed on rusty hinges, and the boy disappeared inside. The father followed after at a leisurely pace.

Tom turned to Jake. "Think we ought to go warn 'em? Wouldn't want the little one to get hurt."

Jake growled.

"Yeah," Tom grunted and got to his feet. "C'mon."

***

David turned and called to the small boy. "Come along, Jake, there's something I want to show you."

"What is it, daddy?"

"You'll see." He stopped and bent at the waist. "Gotta take your shoes off first."

"Why?"

"It's tradition."

"What's... addition?"

David tousled his son's hair. "It's a special thing we always do."

Father and son went, barefoot, across the field.

"Ooh, cool barn," said Jake. He took off at a run. "I wanna see."

David sighed and shrugged. There was time. He called out a fatherly caution. "Watch for nails, son, and don't climb into the loft."

He followed after his son, stripping petals from a picked wildflower.

A shriek from the boy sent him running. "Jake? Are you all right?"

David jerked the barn door open, receiving several splinters in his hand from the dry wood, and rushed inside. Sunlight slanted in through gaps in the barnwood illuminating dust motes and abandoned spider webs.

Jake stood below the hayloft, looking dazed but unhurt. Fragments of hay showered down from a hole in the loft floor.

David knelt and took his son by the arms. "What happened?"

A single tear cut a trail through the dust and dirt on Jake's cheek. "Daddy, I'm sorry. I wanted to see."

David looked up and the breath caught in his throat. The floor of the loft gaped from a fresh break in the aged planks. "You were in the loft? Did you fall through?"

Jake nodded. Tears streamed. "The boards broke."

David ran his hands over his son, checking for any injury. No blood. Thank God.

"You're okay?"

Jake nodded. "The man caught me." He smiled. "He had a dog."

David stood. "What man?"

Jake turned and pointed out the door toward the creek. "He went that way." He laughed. "The dog's name was Jake, too. He licked my face."

David went to the door and peered out – no one there. He turned back to his son. "Are you sure? I didn't see anyone leave the barn."

Jake nodded. "I promise, daddy. Look." He pointed at something on the dirt floor.

David went back where Jake pointed and felt the blood drain from his face.

Footprints

Pressed into the inch-deep dirt were the twin, bare footprints of a grown person and pawprints of a large dog. Jake's numerous impressions marred the soil a short distance away, allowing David to track his son's progress through the barn like a Family Circus child's neighborhood trek.

But he could only find the one set of grown prints.

David picked Jake up and backed out of the barn.

Across the field, near the creek where his father's cairn, and that of the dog, resided, David thought he caught a glimpse.

R.L. Keck has been writing fiction for thirty years and has six self-published titles and several short stories to his credit. He lives in the Tampa Bay area with his wife and two Scottish Terriers.

A Fading Image

Have you ever wondered what your life is worth?
What you'll leave as substance when gone from this earth?

For some, it's so easy; they've so much to say.
Accomplishments flourish, in many a way.

For me – not so easy, at this time of life;
I sit and I ponder the joys and the strife.

Are my footprints fading? That's something I fear.
I won't be remembered by those I hold dear.

My life's been quite normal, good times and the bad,
But nothing seems worthy. What "greats" have I had?

I've raised me a couple of boys, to be proud,
And sent them off wanting to surpass the crowd.

I've done what I could and helped those who have less,
And tried not to settle in giving my best.

The years after cancer when life seemed unsure,
Convinced there's a reason for all we endure.

So, what is the answer? What's left now to do?
Define the term "greatness." I don't have a clue.

I haven't been famous, with no special skills,
But always a worker and that paid the bills.

Not much of a dancer, couldn't sing worth a lick,
No radiant beauty, nor someone's great pick.

I did not spend money. I always made due.

Footprints

And as for temptations, I wrestled a few.

Is there pride in pursuing a lesser cause?
Are we bound by the gifts that give others pause?

The times when life hands you a cross you can't bear,
I tried to remember that others need care.

I measured up quickly and handled it all.
When times called for action, I tried not to fall.

Could it be resilience in facing these trials?
That helped keep me going and chalked up the miles?

That calm steady spirit should count for a lot.
I didn't always see it or else I forgot.

No fanfare, no drama, I just did my bit.
Was there any warmth in the fires I lit?

If there when you're needed, perhaps that's enough.
For those who'll remember, I had the right stuff!

 **Alice Klaxton**, a former schoolteacher, moved to Florida to enjoy the sunshine and her retirement.

The First Step

The first step of my healing
was to acknowledge loss.
A well-meaning friend
welcomed me to a club
she had hoped I would
never join—like Groucho,
I had never desired to be
a member of any group
that would wish to accept me.

The widows' club astounds,
touching every culture,
cruelly defying every age.
The only requirement is
that excruciating first step:
the bitter acknowledgement
that one has abruptly resumed
her single life and should
bravely, gracefully conform.

Endless waves of grief enabled
me to embrace these women.
Our bonds were universal,
shaped by sorrow, strengthened
by the rawness of our recognition
that we had to forge mechanisms
that would allow us to seize
our lives and honor them before
they slowly withered on the vine.

My widow-sisters cherish memories
and the divine grace that allows
our incapacitating pain to ebb.
The terror of the night still beckons

but now there is hope that we,
who have taken the steps toward
independence and wholeness, will
create the footprints for others
to redefine themselves and survive.

Linda Kraus has taught
university courses in literature and
film studies. She has published
poetry in several literary journals
and anthologies and is currently
editing two collections of poems.
She is an orchid judge, a film
festival judge, a rock hound, and
an impassioned Wagnerian.

A Good Man

Footprints can tell a lot about a man, my father once told me, like—the length of his stride, his shoe size and style, his weight, if he hurried or poked along, or if he stood still, ran, or dragged a leg behind him.

"Most importantly," Pop said, "his footprints show if he's a good man."

I didn't understand what he meant, but I believed him.

***

Chilly February winds whooshed through open car windows as my father and I headed to my uncle's cabbage farm, situated outside our small Florida town. The crop had reached its peak, and my mother asked us to pick a fat cabbage for supper.

With country music booming from the radio, Pop thumped rhythmically on the driver-side door with his left hand and twiddled a cigarette between fingers on his right while steering.

"How's my girl?" he hollered.

"Good, Pop."

"Huh? Speak up."

I muttered a faint response.

"Oh…," he said. "You're foolin' with me." His belly-laugh humbled other noises.

Pop turned onto a narrow country road flanked by cabbage fields. He parked on a grassy shoulder and flicked his cigarette butt out the window. Afterward, he gathered picnic supplies from the glove compartment.

"Set these on the hood," he instructed. "And stay on the grass."

I exited the car and watched Pop slowly plod into rich farmland soil. Dirt clods stuck to his black dress shoes—spit-polished each night. I thought back to Pop's saying about footprints; he spoke of solid steps, carefully placed and steady.

I then laid out the supplies he'd handed me: paper napkins, a folded kitchen towel, and a salt canister.

The canister's label displayed a smiling, cherub-faced girl strolling in the rain. She looked about my age, seven. I rolled the canister along the car hood, and the salt-girl appeared to run fast in the rain. I imagined myself as the girl.

"Hey!" Pop called out. "How 'bout this big boy for tonight?"

"Uh huh," I said from my dream-fog.

"And looky here!" he said. "A peewee for our snack."

He withdrew a double-blade Case knife from a pants pocket. The knife had belonged to his grandfather.

***

A day earlier, I sat with Pop at his garage workbench while he honed the knife's blades on an Arkansas stone.

"Always take care of your knife," he told me.

Once sharpened, he folded the blades into their carved bone handle and passed the knife and a chamois into my hands to distract me.

"Polish 'er up good," he said, and then swiveled his high-back chair away from me.

I heard a metal workbench-drawer slide open and the telltale rustle of a paper bag stashed inside. Pop's drawer-visits often prompted intense late-night arguments between my parents. I always feared sleep until quiet returned.

I polished the knife until the drawer squeaked shut. Pop spun back to me, cleared his throat, and wiped a hand across wet stained lips. I handed back the knife. He looked it over and winked.

***

Pop opened the knife's longest blade from its handle. He squatted beside the flower-shaped cabbage, lifted its rubbery foliage, and freed the plant from its thick fibrous stem. He stripped off the outer leaves and left them in the field. The peewee met the same fate.

He carried the cabbages to the car and placed them on the towel. Then he sliced the peewee into wedges and passed a salted wedge and a napkin to me. He wiped his knife clean.

"Just one, my girl," he said. "We can't ruin your supper."

We crunched our sweet treat beneath a cloudless sky. Pop shared stories about growing up a mischief-seeking farm boy. He chuckled as I demonstrated my salt-canister trick on the car hood. And we laughed when crows scuffled over the leaves he'd discarded in the field.

As we packed up, I glanced back at Pop's footprints. I pictured them sunbaked into the field forever.

***

A week later, picking season ended.

Pop visited the workbench-drawer too many times that week, my mother said. Loud voices volleyed between them one afternoon. Doors slammed.

Pop entered my room and shushed me.

"Let's go to the farm," he whispered. Liquor breath betrayed him.

I shook my head, but he urged me along. I relented.

Mother ran alongside the car, pounding clinched fists against the driver-side window. I glimpsed a vivid red mark on her cheek and panic in her eyes.

"Leave her here!" she screamed.

I grabbed for the door handle, but Pop stomped the gas pedal. We sped off toward the farm.

His hands gripped the steering wheel and lips pinched tight on a cigarette.

Though confused and afraid, I denied tears.

Tires screeched when he swerved onto the country road. The car slid sideways along the grassy shoulder where he'd parked for our picnic. He opened his window, cut the engine, and lit another cigarette. While he smoked it and then another down to nubs, I peered out at the field.

The previous week, sage-green cabbage crops had spread across the fields like a knobby hand-crocheted blanket. Today, harvest remnants lay strewn among bare furrows of fresh plowed muck.

Pop reached across me and jerked open the glove compartment. I flinched.

He flung about contents, seemingly desperate to find a needed object. The salt canister dropped to the floor-mat. The salt-girl rocked forward, backward, and stopped—nowhere to run.

He located a half-full whiskey pint and clutched it to his chest.

I sat rigid, afraid to move, speak, or cry.

Pop swigged hard on the bottle, like a hungry calf on its mother's teat. Honey-colored liquid seeped from mouth corners and dribbled onto his starched Oxford-cloth shirt.

After drinking the last drop, he lobbed the bottle out the window. It hit the dirt with a thud. I dared a look. The bottle had landed upright, a grave-marker of sorts. It rested where Pop's footprints had recorded a different man a week earlier.

What would his footprints say about him on this day?

My heart flip-flopped listening to Pop slur nonsensical outbursts. He then sat quietly before removing his grandpa's knife from his pants pocket.

He cradled the handle in his hand, buffed it on his sleeve, and tucked it back into his pocket.

"Someday, I'll disappear," he said. "All you'll get back from me is a bag of bones."

***

My parents divorced. Pop moved out of state and endured hard times.

He wrote infrequent letters. I answered every one.

Thirty-five years later, I arranged Pop's flight home. A manila envelope and garment bag accompanied him—his only belongings sent along from a men's shelter.

In the envelope, I found my first-grade photo, my letters, his grandpa's knife and Pop's death certificate.

Long-held tears spilled.

I unzipped the garment bag. Inside were a threadbare sport-coat, a shirt, pants, and worn-down black dress shoes—polished.

I hugged Pop's shoes to my heart.

My thoughts drifted to good times buffing his grandpa's knife and eating our cabbage wedges. I remembered his footprints set firmly into the earth that day.

I wondered what they'd say about him now.

But I knew.

They'd reveal the footprints of...a good man.

Joan Levy has had stories published in five Florida Writers Collection anthologies. Numerous stories have won Royal Palm Literary Awards. Levy is co-founder of the talented Seminole County Writers Short Story Critique Group. Levy's story is dedicated to her Pop, a good man.

Over There

"Let's go!"

The young man of twenty climbed and ran. Void of any cognitive thought, he responded to the command as he had many times before. His destination was, over there. The rain had stopped a short while ago. It was almost the middle of November, he had lost his coat somewhere in the trench, his boots were torn, cold, and wet. Running robotically, avoiding the wood stumps and makeshift blinds. But most of all, circumventing the barbed wire strung across his path, like steel-rolled fences. Jumping over human bodies and weapons left behind. Then more and more bodies, this time there was also a plethora of mutilated horses intertwined with parts of soldiers' corpses. This was the terror and fear that he encountered on his first over-the-top experience.

Up the ladder and over the top to the field, aware of being exposed when he left the safety of the trench, that fear had long ago subsided. He just did it mechanically, knowing that one day he would be one of those crumpled bodies scattered about. Artillery rounds exploding in some sort of pattern all around him. He dodged the craters caused by the cannons, and continued to run to, over there. He jumped over the wire and tripped into a hole, but quickly regained his fast run forward.

A light rain fell, drove down, hitting him in his face. Steam appeared, which came out all over the youth's body. His body had become overheated from the long run he had made. It was a welcome feeling at the right time.

The young man, named Joe, picked up his step and ran faster towards, over there. A positive feeling came over him, his long limbs burst with the feeling of youth. He jumped higher than before. He ran around the debris, with the skill of a quarter horse who had to cut out a steer from a herd. There was no stopping his courageous charge toward, over there. Men are made of blood and muscle, skin and bone, as much as they may feel like iron, they are not.

A loud thunderous boom, and a flash of fire, hit nearby Joe's path. The explosion and its following concussion jarred and rattled his head, as a force of burning hot wind knocked him down. Confused and disoriented, he opened his eyes, not knowing how long he had been out. He moved his arms and reached down to his legs, everything seemed to be intact, except his boots. The heels had been blown off. Very deliberately, removed the vestiges of what once were boots off his feet. They served him well, he had walked hundreds of miles with them. He carefully moved slow, as he got up on his knees. Then he picked himself up from the slippery mud, continued to move forward. Unable to hear any sounds and his eyes blurred, he sustained his footslog. Thoughts ran unrestrained in his head. Crazy thoughts, of home and family

The young man had been truant from home for a year now. The last time at home, he was a Member of the Rainbow Division, The Fighting Sixty-Ninth. He was dressed up in his US Army Calvary uniform, wearing jodhpurs, with brand new shiny riding boots. He recalled the day he kissed mom good bye. Turned to his dad and hugged him, "I hope I will make you proud!"

"I know you will!"

His father had fought bravely in several of the many European wars. When Joe played with his dad's uniform, which fit him well except for his father's boots, they were much too big for Joe's feet, his dad would reassure him. "Don't worry, someday, well, someday!"

His father tried to appear stoic, even with a tear in his eye, "Joe, come back safe!"

He thought families must have gone through a similar farewell when they left their relatives back in Europe to come to America. Ironically, he would be going back, over there. It was a happy day for the youth. The journey he was about to embark upon, over there, was waiting for him. Tall for the time, just under six feet, a recent high school graduate, a gal who would wait for him. He felt he had it all, especially all the answers to life. This signified he was a man, didn't have to wait for two additional years to turn twenty-one.

These thoughts faded in and out of his head. Fresh thoughts captivated his consciousness. Sometime last year, the Army needed more infantry than calvary soldiers because of the death rate of horses. Now here he was running on his feet and not hoofs. Thought back to days on the battlefield, when the sweet and foul scents rose, with a green smoke-like ambiance in the air. The pain he sustained due to the injuries from his leg and skull.

Sent by ambulance to a hospital tent, inundated by suffering men, many amputees, surrounded by screams and blood. His mind had brought an awareness to the horrors he had seen and experienced in the last year. Remembered that many of his newly-acquired friends no longer walked this earth. Their faces no longer torn and ripped by the barbed wire. For them, no more gagging on the green gas called phosgene. No more being deprived of fresh air, just choking, burning and screaming from mustard gas. He had heard so much screaming, crying, begging, that it became moot.

He didn't hear a thing anymore, nor did he notice hundreds of bodies, torn and grotesquely splayed, all over the field which encircled him. Without boots to protect his feet, he slowed his pace down, but still focused ahead, over there. Far upon the horizon, there were flashes, matching the flares above him. He heard no sounds, the air smelled fresher than he could remember. The night sky was clear with blinking stars. The young soldier's bare feet were sliding on the greasy mud. It actually had a nice, smooth, slippery feeling. At this moment he realized he was dead.

For once, there was no sound around him nor pain in or on his body, he had the sensation of floating. The cloud he was about to slide through in front of him had an image hard to decipher. He was sure it was an angel. The image came through the smoky cloud and spoke. The hearing loss he had experienced from the explosion was wearing off.

The angel said, "You can go home now, Yank, the war was over this morning, at the eleventh hour, the eleventh day, of the eleventh month."

It was a smiling Brit that was his angel. The date was November 11, 1918, Armistice Day. His mom and dad greeted him at the pier. He kissed his mom and hugged his father. No longer over there! Now he is over here!

"One minute, son, I brought something here for you."

"Dad, they're your boots," as he slipped into a pair, of perfectly fitting boots.

"See son, this is the someday I always knew would come. Your feet finally filled my shoes! For what you have accomplished, your footprints are larger than mine."

Richard Lipari wrote articles for WNYF when he was an active New York City Firefighter. He is a world traveler, with numerous hobbies from model airplanes to motorcycles and RVing. Richard is a passionate cook. He enjoys life in St. Augustine, FL with his wife, Lucy.

Yellow Footprints

We traveled all through the night.
First by train then by bus,
for many their first train ride if you rule out the subway.

It was a long tedious journey
through one state after another, after another, then another,
arriving just as night expressed its last vestige of darkness
and began a slow fade to white.

Dawn's early light, day's rebirth,
and soon to find out ours as well…the timing was symbolic.

Peaking from the window of the bus
I saw rows of yellow footprints painted on the concrete in the distance.
Curious.

Bus airbrakes hissed, then screeched assaulting the silence
and announcing our arrival to fluttering sleepy eyes.
This was our alarm clock for the new day.

Suddenly.
Accordion doors sprang open simultaneously in the front and back of the
bus.
Angry screaming men wearing Smokey Bear hats stormed through the open
doors barking and snarling orders.

"OUT OF THE BUS! OUT OF THE BUS!
OUT OF THE GODDAMN BUS!
NOW!
MOVE IT! MOVE IT! MOVE IT!
FASTER! FASTER! FASTER!"

Ambushed by sudden sound and activity, inert bodies stumbled into action
and into each other trying to flee this assault, like wildebeest fleeing

attacking lions.

Some fell into the narrow center isle as our group tried to evacuate
the confining carcass of the bus,
which now began to excrete its bowels onto the tarmac.

Salty, sodden, South Carolina air spit in our faces
as we jumped from the doorways of the vehicle.

"Line-up on the yellow footprints!
DO IT! DO IT NOW!"

"On the yellow footprints!
STAND AT ATTENTION!

DO IT…DO IT NOW!"

We ran towards the footprints, but not fast enough, never fast enough!

They nipped at our heels.
We were herded as hyenas herd their prey.
Some stumbled or fell.
Several Smokies pounced upon them to motivate them back into the herd.

Finally arriving on the footprints no one moved.
No one spoke.
A moment of deafening silence…

Then from the precipice of Hell,
a lone booming voice addressed us.

"Welcome to Paris Island—Marine Recruit Training Depot.
You low-life worthless pieces of whale shit!"

Anthony Malone answered a question when in
sixth grade. "What do you want to be?" He wrote,
Soldier or Artist. After high school he joined the
military. There was a war on. Then came art school.
He became an editorial artist communicating with
pictures. Now he creates images in your mind.

Sole Tracker

I walked into the police station lobby laden with my equipment and thankful for the automatic door. The civilian at the reception desk gave me a nod and buzzed me in.

"How are you doing, Dani?" she asked me.

"Good. Do you know where Detective Roberts wants me this morning?"

She dropped her smile. "Interview three."

I walked toward the back of the station and saw Officer Stephanie Williams. She had her brown hair pulled into a bun, but the shorter strands hung in disarray around her face. She looked as if she hadn't slept in days.

I gave her a nod. "Morning, Williams."

"Dani." She nodded and pointed to the interview room.

Once in the room, I set up my computer on the table and placed the scanner on the floor. When I first started in this business, no one was eager to hire my services. But, as crime increased along with my success rate in finding the perpetrators, police departments in the Florida Panhandle hired me with greater regularity. I heard the door open but didn't look up.

"Hi, Dani." I recognized Detective Roberts' voice. "I brought Sergeant Collins to meet you."

I stood up and faced a fiftyish man with a white bushy mustache. I extended my hand, "Daniella De Luca, sir."

He grabbed my hand in a sturdy grip. "Anthony Collins. Nice to meet you. Roberts tells me you helped him solve three cases in as many weeks."

I smiled and nodded.

"Being the new man on the team here, I'm getting a feel for operations. You know. How we investigate, etc." His gravelly voice trailed off.

"Are you familiar with this new technology?" I pointed to the scanner on the floor.

"Heard about it. We didn't use it where I came from. Old fashioned, I guess."

"Well, I hope you can stick around to see it in action, Sergeant."

Roberts took a step toward me. "We have three people of interest, Dani, and they're all here. Just tell me when you're set."

"Give me another five minutes."

Roberts and Collins turned and left the room. One table, four chairs, a two-way mirror, and a camera mounted in the corner. Pretty dull place. I knew Roberts and Collins would be in the small observation room behind the mirror, so I gave a thumbs up to signal I was ready.

Officer Williams escorted a young woman into the room. Twenties, attractive, casually dressed. Williams handed me a five-by-eight card with Number One written for the name. I told them I didn't want to know names, so the police assigned the suspects numbers.

Number One kept looking at Williams and then back at me. "What's going on? Who are you?" she asked me.

"I'm Dani DeLuca. I assist the police with their investigations. Please, take off your shoes."

"My shoes? What the hell's going on?"

Williams closed the door and leaned against the wall behind Number One.

"This is a scanner." I pointed to the square blue panel on the floor. "When you were born, the hospital fitted you, well, all of us, with a microchip on the bottom of your foot. When you stand on the scanner, it can tell us where you've been for the last forty-eight hours."

Number One protested. "That microchip was designed to help our parents find us if we were kidnapped. It didn't track our comings and goings."

"Originally, yes. But today, those chips act like the GPS on your car."

She crossed her arms. "I won't do it."

Williams stepped next to Number One. "Refusal could be used against you in court."

"Will the results be shared with my husband?"

"Oh, my, no," I said, holding back a chuckle. "As long as you weren't near the location in question at the time of the crime, these results are not shared with anyone."

Number One removed her shoes and stood on the scanner. I pressed the green button, which started the scanner to hum and photograph her soles. When the light reached her heel, my computer lit up with a list of latitude and longitude numbers and the dates and times for each coordinate. I hit the print button.

"Can I see it?" She pointed her chin toward the printout.

"Sure." I handed the paper to her but knew the list of numbers would be meaningless.

"This is dumb." She tossed the paper on the table and looked at Williams. "Am I done here?"

"Please follow me, ma'am. It won't be long."

While I waited for the next suspect, I disinfected the scanner and prepared the computer for Number Two.

This time, a very large man followed Williams into the room. His rumpled clothes looked as if he had slept in them. It appeared he hadn't combed his hair in a week either, and there was an odor of garlic that reached my nose from three feet away.

I started my usual spiel when he interrupted and said, "This is a joke. I haven't been anywhere near the Seven-Eleven. Harassment. Nothing but harassment."

"If you haven't been there, this should prove it." I explained the scanner and what it would do, whereupon Number Two speedily took off his shoes and socks and a nauseating smell permeated the room.

When I completed the scan, I sent him out of the room, and immediately applied disinfectant to the equipment. I wished I had a room deodorizer.

It didn't take long for Williams to bring in Number Three. A slim man, around mid-twenties. He had a tightly cropped beard that matched his short black hair. He didn't say a word but sat down to remove his shoes and socks.

"This scanner will tell us where you've been…" I started.

"Yes. I know."

"You've been through this procedure before? I don't remember you."

"Why should you? You look at feet all day, not faces."

He was right. I always said one look at a person's feet and I knew everything.

After I scanned Number Three, Collins and Roberts entered the room.

Collins smiled. "You don't want to know their names. Hell, you don't even want to know the crime."

"I prefer it that way."

The Sergeant pointed to the papers. "Anything?"

I handed the stack to him. "Now you and Roberts get to chart their movements."

I walked to my car knowing which of the three was guilty of something but not from their location coordinates. In the last six months, my sole tracker had evolved, almost like a virus mutates. I could see more than latitude and longitude points. The first time I captured a bluish flame on the screen I thought my computer malfunctioned. But it happened consistently now. Blue flames, dark red flames, and even purple flames. They're rather like a person's aura. I've come to realize that I not only track their movements, I also get a glimpse into their souls. The darker the flame, the more sinister the soul. I don't need names, but I do keep records. They might come in handy someday.

Arleen Mariotti is a retired teacher. She has published three textbooks, numerous articles, and several short stories. She is currently an adjunct instructor at HCC, and volunteers to teach art at senior living facilities.

Angel Baby

The crash of the Choctaw Flyer passenger train on its trip from Oklahoma City to Tulsa made the six o'clock evening news. Bold headlines in *The Morning Register* newspaper blared: TRAIN CRASH: 199 Dead. The article described how passengers and attendants were crushed beneath the train that sped 115 miles an hour when it left the rails, spun in mid-air, and landed in a soggy marsh—a snake-like metallic corpse mangled and twisted with plumes of smoke announcing its demise. The report indicated one lone survivor, a four-month old baby boy. Swaddled in a blue blanket, wearing small, Indian-beaded booties and a Winnie-the-Pooh jumper, he looked up and smiled at the firemen as they lifted him off a damp grassy patch.

At the city hospital, his baby footprints were recorded. Chief Emergency Room Doctor Tracy Darren examined every inch of his small body for broken bones, bleeding, and bruises then scheduled him for an internal injury CT scan. At 11:55 p.m., prior to departing and somewhat perplexed, Dr. Tracy approached the head nurse.

"Are these reports the train baby's? Perhaps his got mixed up with another patient's."

The nurse said, "No. That's the entire medical report of the train-wreck baby. Why? What's wrong?"

"Wrong?" Tracy's eyebrows shot high. "Nothing's wrong. That's the problem. The baby is perfectly healthy. No broken bones, no bruises, no nothing." She tilted her head and gave a grateful smile. "I think we have a miracle baby on our hands."

On her way out, she peered into the window of the baby room. The tiny patient slept soundly. The nurse in charge had prepared a label for his crib: Angel Baby.

But things got stranger.

Soon after arriving to her post the next day, she learned that first responders had uncovered an aged couple still alive and buried beneath the wreckage. Dr. Tracy visited the baby room and asked the attending nurse about the condition of "Angel Baby."

"He's fine. He ate a good breakfast and finished a bottle to boot. Gonna be a big one, that one," she jested.

Dr. Tracy entered the baby room for a quick examination of Angel Baby. "Hey, Angel Baby, you have two more survival buddies. They found them last night." She smiled.

The baby boy looked directly into her eyes and broke into a big toothless grin as though he understood. Angel Baby's parents still remained a mystery. A full investigation of crash victims had begun, but the doctor learned no one evidenced kinship with the baby.

Over the next two days, Dr. Tracy grew fond of Angel Baby and at one point cradled him in her arms. She felt an attachment, and with no marriage looming in the immediate future, her mothering genes took the initiative. She rocked Angel Baby and talked to him, again reporting the good news about surviving passengers and telling him how lucky he was.

"We're still searching for your parents, Angel Baby. We'll find them, I promise." A happy cooing sound left his puckered mouth, followed by that infectious grin.

With no identification of the baby's parents confirmed, he remained in the hospital but was designated for possible placement at a foster child agency. News continued to roll in. Three more victims of the train crash were found alive under collapsed cabin ceilings. Oddly, none had serious injuries, mostly bruises and minor cuts. Dr. Tracy brought Angel Baby the good news. Angel Baby's bright smile broke out again; his eyes twinkled and his little legs kicked faster than a dog's wagging tail. At one point, after being told of new survivors, he reached up and touched the doctor's cheek. She shed a tear at the contact. It fell onto his finger which he placed in his mouth.

Thinking that Angel Baby's bright persona would be an asset in the emergency room, Dr. Tracy, asked for and received permission to keep him in the emergency area to ease the emotional trauma of incoming patients. While the investigation to identify his parents continued. the doctor transferred him to the emergency room each night upon her arrival, and the rate of emergency recoveries increased significantly. And when she returned him to his crib, she thanked him with a hug and a kiss for his magic.

"Folks are healing better and faster, Angel Baby," she said. She waited for that angelic smile and listened for his baby sounds of approval.

The chief cardiologist, Dr. Rubin, learned of Angel Baby's effect in the ER and asked the hospital administration if the baby, properly swathed, could be present in the operating room to allay the fears of cardio patients for surgery. And so it was, with similar results, patient post-operative survival rates increased and recovery times improved dramatically.

One night while rocking Angel Baby in her arms, Dr. Tracy asked him, "Who are you, my Angel? Is it love that patients see on your face?"

He wiggled in her arms, wound his little fingers around her pinky, then flashed his magic, toothless smile.

That did it. Dr. Tracy decided if no one claimed Angel Baby, she would adopt him. The soul to soul contact with this little Angel was so binding she felt it was inevitable, carved in the mystery of her own life.

On a day before her scheduled vacation, Dr. Tracy visited with the hospital director and asked if she was allowed to proceed with adopting the baby since no one claimed him.

"Oh, but that's not so," he said. "He left the hospital this morning in the arms of his parents—a young couple, two of the train survivors who thought they had lost their child in the collision. After they provided proper documentation, we released the baby into their charge. He's in very loving hands."

Dr. Tracy left the hospital feeling thankful but disappointed.

After her vacation, Dr. Tracy decided to visit Angel Baby to check on his recovery. In the process of tracking down his address, she discovered his entire medical file was missing—except for a copy of his footprints. Odd, she thought, but nonetheless prepared for the visit. A young man answered the door when she knocked, with a woman, presumably his wife, in the background.

Dr. Tracy introduced herself and described her role during his son's hospitalization after the train accident. "I'm just following up on his progress."

He looked at her, his face a blank. "We don't have a child, miss, and we've never been in a train accident. You must have the wrong address," he said and slammed the door shut.

Dejected, Dr. Tracy headed for her car as it began to rain. She placed her briefcase over her head. But as she reached for the door handle she removed her hand and lowered her briefcase. Turning to the sky, she let the falling rain splash down on her face, suddenly realizing there never were parents on the wrecked train, not even at the hospital—only an Angel Baby with no medical file —only footprints left to the world.

"Thank you," she said to a clearing in the clouds. "Thank you for your Baby Angel." She smiled and headed to the hospital for her shift.

Frank T. Masi has short stories published in FWA's Collections, *The Florida Writer*, and *Not Your Mother's Book…On Working for a Living*. Frank's poetry is in FSPA's *Cadence, Revelry, and Poets of Central Florida*. He edited the non-fiction book *The Typewriter Legend*, published business articles, and won poetry awards.

Celeste

For two days, the news featured the multiple car crash on I-70 near Frederick, Maryland, showing aerial views of the accident from every angle. They partly blamed the first snowfall of the season as the cause.

Olivia's life crashed too. She had stayed home that day while her husband and her mother ran errands in town. They had been returning home on the interstate when a semi-trailer truck lost control and rear-ended their car. A chain reaction resulted involving nine vehicles—three persons killed and many injured.

Olivia's forty-year-old husband died in the collision. Her mother, Esther, suffered numerous fractures and lay comatose at Frederick Memorial Hospital. In her late seventies, Esther's doctors cautioned Olivia not to expect a recovery. Yet on the twelfth day, Esther woke up.

As soon as Olivia received the phone call that her mother was awake, she arranged with a babysitter to stay with her two young children while she went to the hospital. When she entered her mother's room, a woman about Olivia's age stood by the bed, talking and stroking Esther's head in a soothing manner.

"Excuse me, do you work here? Do you know my mother?"

"I used to be a nurse. Today, I was visiting someone on this floor and heard this lady came out of her coma. So, I had to check on her. Force of habit, I guess." She gave Esther's hand a gentle squeeze and said to Olivia, "I'll leave you with your mother."

Olivia's tone mellowed. "Well . . . thanks for coming by."

Alone with her mother, Olivia hugged her. Esther stared off into space, unable to focus. "Mom, I'm so glad you're back. You'll be fine now. The kids miss you so much." When Olivia spoke, she glanced at her, but her face was expressionless. No words came out.

Day after day Olivia went to see Esther, and each time, the woman she now knew as Celeste was there. Olivia could not shake an indefinable, unsettled feeling. Stopping at the nurses' station, she asked, "Have you seen a woman in my mother's room every afternoon? She's average height, with light brown hair in a braid. Probably in her early forties."

"Your mother . . . room 206, right?" The nurse thought for a moment. "No, I can't say for sure. We've been so busy." She turned and asked the young assistant engaged in paperwork at the counter behind her. "Marion, has there been a woman visiting in 206?"

"Hmm, maybe . . . hard to say. So many people come and go," Marion said.

Although disturbed that no one else had noticed Celeste's presence, Olivia was grateful for her visits. She had a positive effect on her mother. Esther was becoming more alert and able to articulate simple words, mostly yes and no.

"You have the magic touch, Celeste. I can tell my mother enjoys your company."

"It's reassuring to a patient out of a coma to have somebody talk to them. I'm happy to be of help."

"Celeste, why aren't you working as a nurse anymore, if you don't mind my asking? You're not old enough to be retired."

"I'll get back to it someday. Right now, let's just say I'm between jobs."

As the days passed, dark circles appeared under Olivia's once bright eyes. Known to be an energetic person, now her posture sagged. The daily trips to the hospital and looking after her children and the farm were wearing her down.

She approached Celeste with an offer. "My mother will be discharged before long. Her doctor believes she can continue convalescing at home. The truth is, insurance won't cover extended hospitalization." Olivia's brow creased. "I'm in a real bind here, Celeste. She needs full-time care. I have children and a farm to run on my own since my husband passed. I can't pay much, but would you be interested in working as her caregiver?"

"Tell you what, Olivia, you provide me with room and board, and that'll be enough pay for me."

"Are you serious?" Gratitude lit her eyes. "You're a godsend, Celeste!"

***

Close to Frederick, Olivia's small farm sat among the hills in the rural town of Myersville, quite a distance from the main highway, accessible only by a long, narrow gravel road. The morning she brought her mother home, a brooding sky sprinkled sufficient snow to cover everything in white. She prepared a room for Celeste and waited. It was almost dark and there was no sign of her. Disturbing thoughts cluttered Olivia's mind: maybe she had an accident driving on the icy road . . . or didn't she say a friend would drop her off? Or did she? Perhaps she changed her mind . . .

The sound of a couple knocks lifted her spirits. She ran to answer the door.

Celeste stood on the front porch, snowflakes still attached to her hair and the shoulders of her coat. "Sorry, I got delayed."

Olivia breathed a sigh of relief. "Goodness, did you walk all the way up the lane? Your friend should have driven you up . . . never mind, please come in and get warm." She took the woman's suitcase and ushered her inside. "You're just in time for dinner."

***

Weeks rolled by. With Celeste's aid and therapy, Esther gained ample strength to push herself around with a walker, and her speech gradually cleared. Neighbors and friends called her recovery "miraculous."

In February, the groundhog's prediction of six more weeks of winter proved correct. One evening, everyone in Olivia's household sat around the kitchen table warming up with some hot cocoa. Celeste put down her cup and drew a deep breath. "Dear ones, it's time for me to go." She faced Esther and patted her hand lying on the table. "You're doing very well, so I'll leave tomorrow morning. My friend will pick me up at the end of the gravel road."

"Oh, no!" said Esther and the children.

Olivia pleaded, "Please, Celeste, can't you stay awhile longer? You're an important member of our family."

"I appreciate your kindness, Olivia, but my job here's done. You'll be fine."

Like in a snow globe, the snow fell quietly throughout that night. In the morning, the white landscape glistened in the sun as if diamond dust had been sprinkled from heaven. In contrast, gloom and sadness filled the house. Olivia and Esther held back their tears, but both children cried openly as they hugged Celeste goodbye.

With Celeste gone, they headed toward the kitchen when Olivia's seven-year-old son, Alex, spotted something in the hall. "Mom, Celeste forgot her suitcase."

"Hurry, get your coat on, grab the suitcase, and catch her. She can't be far."

The boy did as told. But when he opened the door and looked around, he said, "I can't see her anywhere."

"Oh, c'mon, Alex. Nobody walks that fast in the snow. Just follow her footprints. They'll lead you to her."

"But Mom, there are no footprints."

The four of them gathered at the door. As far as the eye could see, no human or animal had yet made their mark on the fresh snow.

Angie M. Mayo is a retired pharmacist, who enjoys having the time to write stories and poems from her home in Hernando, Florida. She is a member of the Freedom Writers Group and the Port Orange Scribes. Presently, working on a collection of anecdotes for her memoir.

Prescription

The first Christmas carol that impressed me was "Good King Wenceslas." I was about five years old when I heard it and I'll never forget the stirring in my heart. I pictured the king by his fireside, when he suddenly noticed, outside in the freezing night, a lone peasant carrying firewood. Moved with compassion, he ventured out to invite the stranger home for a hot meal. His large boots broke a trail through the deep crusted snow and he instructed the weary stranger to follow closely in his footsteps. Legend claims heat rose from the king's footprints as the pauper stepped in them. That demonstration of regal tenderness made an indelible mark on me. The memory, as I grew up, evolved into a longing for someone to go before me, to break a path in areas where I felt overwhelmed. Without quite realizing it, I had a deep inner longing for a mentor.

I was close to my father, a wonderful teacher and guide in my early years, but Dad died before my first book of poetry made it to print. A year later I was introduced to someone who would become a cherished friend for the next three decades, until his death four years ago. At first glance, like the king and the pauper, it would seem I should have had little in common with Professor William Prouty. As a young mother with four children and elderly in-laws consuming my every waking moment, I wasn't up to my neck in snow, but I was certainly immersed in the "family circus." I am not sure what made me think I could write poetry at the time, but I was determined to try. William was an accomplished and devoted professor, head of Humanities at University of New Brunswick in Saint John, and an active participant in literary circles on and off campus. Technically we should have had few shared interests and scant time for each other. But in the wonderful way in which serendipities happen when you are open to them, we delighted in each other's presence from the beginning.

William read my poems, discussed them with me, and made valuable comments and suggestions. Never did he flatter or falsely praise if something wasn't working, but neither was he ever harsh, cruel or condescending. If I sent something off to him in too hasty a fashion, I would likely get the response, "This is okay, but not your best." He would tell me where the poem went off the rails in the third stanza. He was fanatical about punctuation. He also let me know when he was impressed with a piece, and why. Usually I would acquiesce to his suggestions but occasionally, like Humpty Dumpty, I would stick up for my choice of word or phrase. He would smile and say, "Doesn't it feel good to defend your work?" Words of praise from William were coveted and cherished because he always made me work for them. Decades of this attentive one-on-one mentoring greatly influenced my work and challenged me to become a better poet.

In addition to the ways in which William guided and molded my development as a writer, he tramped ahead and broke a trail though the tangled underbrush in many areas of life and parted the bushes for me to view vistas I might never otherwise have witnessed. In my library, many books are gifts received after long conversations in which he would ask if I had read a certain author, or exclaim with enthusiasm that I would love so and so's work. Within days of these animated discussions, parcels wrapped in brown paper, tied with lavender ribbon, and inscribed in William's flowing calligraphic script, would arrive at my door.

As my library was enhanced from his contributions of everything from science fiction to poetry, nature tomes to biographies, so gradually was my garden. As he edited my poems, so he edited my gardens after every walkabout in his bare feet. A corner here, a patch there, could use an addition and he had just the cure. Dozens of exotic day lilies, with petals ranging from pale lemon sorbet and raspberry red to dark grape and vivid apricot, would magically appear from the trunk of his car. Eventually my perennial beds became a profusion of colors and fragrances breathing William's spirit afresh every spring.

Enjoying creativity in multiple areas of our lives, one of our joys was sharing recipes. An absolute gourmet, he traded his delicate "pear-leek bisque" recipe for my hearty "spiced beet chutney." I offered my "oyster mushrooms in Parmesan cheese cups" in exchange for his tangy "spring-time sorrel soup." While he often hosted elaborate dinner parties with his artistically prepared meals, William was equally at ease in my old farmhouse slicing off a slab of homemade bread and freshly roasted turkey and assembling himself a sandwich at my big old wooden table. We chatted and laughed while I continued making green tomato chowchow.

The word that comes to mind when I think of all my interactions with William, is "tenderness." We shared many hours of joy and celebration, but we also trusted each other with our most personal burdens during the more trying seasons of life. I called him when my husband was experiencing a life-threatening heart attack. When he was distraught over his partner's critical illness we emailed, every hour, all night long.

Even from miles away, he found ways to brighten my day, such as during what became known as "the winter of endless snow." After a storm that lasted a whole week and left us buried in almost six feet of snow, I became ill with pneumonia. I had received a "Provincial Creations Grant" to work on my second book, and felt increasingly stressed by imminent deadlines. The children were house-bound for the week and the power went off rendering my computer useless. William called and gave me a kindly lecture to take care of myself. A few days later I traipsed down the driveway to the mailbox. No kingsize boots had broken a trail for me and wet snow chilled my ankles as I reached inside for the brown-papered package tied with lavender ribbon. I discovered a luxurious box of signature chocolate truffles. William's accompanying note was written as a prescription. "Rest every day. Take two truffles every four hours with a cup of tea. Repeat as desired." I did. It cured me!

I am grateful I had a mentor who challenged and inspired me. My life was richer and more enjoyable in multiple fields because of the times he walked ahead of me as well as the times he strolled beside me. I aspire to follow in his footprints and especially emulate his immense tenderness. After all, who would not benefit from a prescription of chocolate truffles?

Phyllis McKinley brought her passion for writing with her when she moved to Florida from New Brunswick, Canada. Recipient of multiple literary awards, and author of five books, Phyllis loves her family and friends and appreciates each moment lived. Her stories appear in seven previous FWA Collections.

Bigfoot Stomping Grounds

Asher picked his way through the Georgia pines, careful to maintain a pace his wife could follow without whining. Granted, the trail up the mountain was steep, and rocky and he felt bad. But he needed her help.

When he turned around he saw his better half clutching her hiking staff like a drowning person.

"What idiot," she panted, "buys a dying, piece of shit *Bigfoot* museum in the middle of the Blue Ridge?"

"*This* idiot—and stop calling me that."

"You just called yourself—never mind. I can't talk to you when you're like this."

"Like what?"

"Possessed. Obsessed. Depressed. A mess. Pick one."

They'd had this exact same argument every few days for the past month. He ignored her, and inhaled deep, with closed eyes. The clean, cold pine scent scrubbed his sinuses and filled his lungs with fresh hope. He held the breath until blood pounded in his temples before exhaling slowly.

"Smell that?" he said.

"You're not a mountain man, Asher. I love you, but you can't fish to feed a cat. The only hunting you've ever done is through want ads. And you couldn't hike your way to the bathroom without GPS."

"You wait. Our museum is going to take off big time. Then, you'll sing a different tune."

"Face it, my darling, that broken down old redneck who sold you his collection of doctored photos and fake eyewitness accounts saw you coming. Siler's Bigfoot Emporium? I guarantee that pathetic tourist trap of his has never turned a profit. Its biggest day had to be two months ago when you forked over ten bucks admission and stumbled through its paint-peeling doors."

"First of all, I changed the name."

"*Bigfoot Stomping Grounds*? Seriously?"

"Laugh all you want."

"I'm not laughing. Trust me."

"Second of all, I have a plan."

"You always have a plan, honey. Remember your Eat Shit line of greeting cards? Or, that god-awful combination pill bottle and iPhone protector? Your glow-in-the-dark dog collars have got to be my favorites, though. Hell, you almost convinced me. Who knew the Chinese used chemicals hazardous to pets? Big dreams, my husband. I used to love you for those. But, big dreams followed close by epic fails? Every time? I'm sorry, but it gets old."

She shook her head and unscrewed the top of a water bottle and drained it. Her third in two hours. Nature ought to be calling her number any time now, which should be interesting.

Their trail ascended the mountain, flirting with the drop-off edge most of the way up, coming close to rocky outcroppings that took his breath whenever he ventured close enough to peek over.

He took pity on her and slung the backpack off his shoulders, massaging where the straps dug in. "You catch your breath. I'm gonna take in the view." He pointed to his pack. "Guard that with your life."

The overlook beckoned and he hopped gingerly from granite shelf to boulder to more granite until he'd climbed out onto a level slab of rock. The Vibram soles of his shiny new hiking boots gripped like Velcro.

Two eagles rode thermals overhead in a royal blue sky. An evergreen panorama enfolded him from either side, blanketing a jagged landscape carved by god. Far below, the valley floor descended a full vertigo-inducing mile, highlighted by a sparkling ribbon of river.

He backed away from the edge to scan ground closer at hand. Patches of soft earth nestled randomly between up-thrust rounds of rock. Perfect. Now, for the plan.

The climb back came easy, fueled by adrenaline. But when he returned, his wife held up the contents of his backpack, eyebrows raised.

"This is part of your plan?"

"Easy with that. Right now it's more valuable than you are."

Faded to the color of old teeth, the aged piece of fiberglass casting was vaguely rectangular, wider at one end. About two feet by one and a half feet, the backside featured a cross-hatched cloth texture, the front held the imprint of a monstrously oversized foot.

"You carried your fake sasquatch footprint all the way up this mountain? I can only imagine what—oh, you have got to be kidding."

"It's called salting the claim, a time-honored tradition among buyers and sellers."

"Among thieves and scoundrels, you mean. Asher you're better than this."

"We're not filling shotgun shells with gold dust and firing into creek banks. We're making a different sort of impression. Drumming up interest in our museum. Where's the harm?"

Footprints

"It's illegal, Asher. Not to mention plain wrong."

"It's *not* illegal. Besides, is Bigfoot real?" Asher shrugged. "People believe what they want to believe. Old Man Siler claimed that footprint came from somewhere in these mountains. I'm merely bringing it home to see its kin. Thing is though, I'm gonna need your help."

"You're kidding."

"We'll have to jump on that casting together. Bigfoot's huge. One person won't weigh enough to convince anyone. Our combined weight will make it authentic."

Two sweaty hours later Asher leaned against a shady oak. "Last one, baby. I swear. People come by here all the time for the views. We're giving them one more thing to look at, that's all."

He spotted a clearing down the trail a ways, a well-used campsite complete with smoke-blackened fire ring. Bingo.

"Why don't you scout out that piece of dirt over there? I'll even let you choose our final spot."

"You are so going to owe me, Asher Clements." She marched off, kicking at clumps of pine needles and leaves. Nearer the campsite she slowed, head down, studying the ground. Then she froze.

Asher barely noticed, listening intently for approaching hikers. Nothing. In fact, everything had gone eerily silent and still. Gave him a bit of the willies truth be told and he shivered. He covered that moment of weakness by twisting out of his pack and extracting the footprint

"Asher? *Asher!*"

"What?"

"As God is my witness, you are losing your freaking mind."

"I told you, darling. This is the last one—."

"That's not it. Look," she pointed at the ground, "we've already been here. I must be losing my mind, too, because I didn't remember either. Must be all this damn fresh air."

He walked over, shaking his head. "Not possible. We started up the trail and worked our way down—oh, shit."

That earlier creepy feeling trailed icy fingers down his spine. He looked up, still as stone, swiveling his head slowly.

"Gimme that. I'll prove it." She snatched the plaster print from his hands and laid it beside the fresh impression in the dirt. "See? A perfect match."

"Except for one thing."

"Why are you whispering?"

"Shh! *Our* foot is a righty. That one—"

He watched blood drain from her face.

"—is a lefty." Her whisper barely moved her lips.

"When I say run—"

The guttural scream came from behind.

It froze his heart and ruffled hairs on his neck.

He watched his wife taking deer leaps down the mountain; ten yards, twelve already. Good girl.

Now, if only his stupid legs would—

Mark McWaters has an MFA in Creative Writing from the University of North Carolina, is an award-winning Advertising Creative Director, a previous #1 and #2 winner in Collections, a multiple RPLA Short Fiction winner and a First Place RPLA winner for unpublished novel in both Thriller and YA categories.

Stubborn Footprints

The front door was unlocked, as promised. I walked into the foyer and called out, "Jerry?"

"In here," came from the living room.

I found Jerry on his knees with a bucket and sponge scrubbing the short pile carpet. When he looked up, the unkind morning light revealed a mess of a man, unshaven, disheveled hair, and wrinkled night shirt hanging open.

"I guess this is why you asked me to bring a carpet cleaner," I said. "But what's the emergency?"

Jerry shook his head. "I really did it this time, buddy."

"What now?" I asked.

"I may be in big trouble with my marriage."

I held my breath.

Jerry continued, "Last evening I was at Willie's Pub. The office was having a farewell party for Gail Mahan. You never met her, but what a looker. After everyone else left, I found myself alone with Gail. We had a couple more drinks and ended up here."

"By here, you mean the house?"

"By here, I mean the bedroom," he replied, with an exaggerated shoulder shrug.

I'd known Jerry and Liz for years. She was attractive and outgoing, but had a mean streak. I knew if she found out about this, she would be more angry than sad. A better description would be furious.

"Where was Liz during all this?" I asked.

Jerry rubbed his temples. "She took her sister out for her birthday and spent the night at her house."

"So you're in the clear."

"No, not exactly. My busybody neighbor, the cul-de-sac sentry, Francis Knitt, saw Gail leaving at 6:30 am. I figure the motion lights alerted her. Anyway, she did me the great favor of calling Liz. I had my phone silenced this morning and later found Liz had called and left me a message that is downright scary. She's surely on her way here right now, driving like a stock car champion."

"Okay, so what's with the scrubbing?"

"Plan A is to simply tell Liz that I had someone deliver urgent paperwork to me early this morning. But that won't explain these." Jerry pointed at two purple footprints on the carpet—high heels. "I've been scrubbing my butt off with no luck."

"I'll get the carpet cleaner," I said as I headed to my car.

The machine sloshed, turned, and steamed for twenty minutes. The footprints were lighter, yet still there. I didn't say anything to Jerry, but it appeared to me the surrounding carpet was a little lighter too.

"How in the world did this happen?" I asked.

"Late last night, Gail and I were drinking wine. I opened another bottle on the kitchen island. When I looked up, Gail was in the bedroom doorway. She summoned me with a finger and disappeared into the bedroom. I was so distracted I knocked over the wine and I wasn't about to clean it up right then. "

"But it's in the living room."

"I know." Jerry seemed impatient with me. "Gail got up in the morning before daylight, got a drink of water in the kitchen and split. She never saw the spilled wine and tracked it from the kitchen onto the carpet. I guess you could say she left me a going away present." He made a sour face.

He half-heartedly ran the cleaner again. After five minutes, he turned it off and shoved it aside in disgust. "Damn it!"

Jerry looked at me wearing desperation and said, "Remember I said Plan A?"

I nodded.

"Well, I have a Plan B."

I held my breath again.

"Do you think you could possibly tell Liz that you spent the night here with Gail?"

I've always followed a simple rule, "Try and do the right thing." That sounds easy when you say it fast, but often when applied, the decision is more difficult than expected. This was one of those times. If I agreed, I would be lying, which usually carries a presumption of being wrong. But if I didn't, I would let down a friend, and risk the end of what I thought was a fine marriage. In searching for the "right thing," should I seek "the greater good"?

Jerry's stare signaled it was my turn to speak. But I didn't want to. There had to be another way to save Jerry. I preferred not to lie to Liz.

"I may not be married, but I'm serious about Sophia, and I shouldn't be fooling around with Gail either," I said.

"That's exactly the reason why you needed to come here with Gail. See, it all fits," Jerry replied, in a tone that beckoned, "Come on, join the conspiracy."

I had the feeling this wouldn't end well, but a friend was asking for help. "Okay," had barely cleared my lips when Jerry sprung to action.

"Come on, we need to stage the guest room," he blurted out, as he grabbed my arm and pulled me along like a bouncer leading a drunk.

He yanked the bedding loose and leaped onto the bed, landing on his back. He then rolled around, flailing his arms and legs like a dying cockroach. Back to his feet, he ran from the room and returned with an open bottle of wine and two glasses. He put them on the night stand.

"What, Gail and I didn't drink any wine?" I asked.

He snatched the bottle and again left and returned. He poured a small amount into each glass, which now emptied the bottle. "There," he said, "you guys polished off one of my best Cabernets. I hope you enjoyed it." Jerry seemed a renewed man, now that he had an escape from his dilemma in place.

"Let's have breakfast, like everything is normal," he said, as he headed toward the kitchen.

After putting eggs in a pan, Jerry scattered a few crackers on the counter. "You and Gail made this mess last night, I'll have you know," he said with an air of panache. I thought maybe he was having too much fun with this.

"So how did I meet Gail?" I asked my accomplice. "You can be sure Liz is going to have some pointed questions for me."

Jerry's stubby-fingered hands stirred the eggs in the pan. "You dropped by the Pub, met her, hit it off, and asked me if you could stay the night here. Liz won't like that I said okay, but I'll gladly take the heat for that instead of, well, you know." Jerry giggled.

"You've got this all worked out, don't you?" I said.

"Hey, if it weren't for those damn stubborn footprints, I'd have been fine."

I heard footsteps as Jerry said, "But with your help, Liz will never be the wiser?"

"So you say!" came from behind me. I turned to see Liz standing at the entrance to the kitchen. Her expression gave me a jolt that surged from my throat to my ass. I did the right thing, at least for me, by slinking out the front door as quickly as I could. My role in the great conspiracy had just been terminated.

George August Meier has won awards for his short stories. His work has appeared in several literary journals. He is a member of the Florida Writers Association and has degrees from Colgate University and The Ohio State University. He and his wife Yvonne reside at the beach in Wilbur-By-The-Sea, Florida.

Side by Side

I leap barefoot off the last worn wooden step onto the pristine seashore. Stumble a bit as my bare feet sink into the damp sand. Land next to you with a thud.

"Knew you'd be here, Anthony," I say, speaking a little more breathlessly than normal. I wonder if anyone could understand us meeting like this.

"Hey, Sarah, which direction today, north or south?" The light of the winter sun kisses your face as your gaze drifts from the ocean to me.

"South. Tide is on the way out. Let's see if we can make it to the jetty."

The wind rustles the sea oats and saw palmettos on the dunes protecting the National Seashore, the salt air a welcome cool after the furnace heat of summer. We wander toward the place where the beach narrows and ends.

"What you looking at, Sarah?"

"You. I still love the look of you."

Your warm open hand rubs my back between the shoulder blades. I wonder how you know it's the exact spot that annoys me today.

"You okay?"

"Yeah, didn't sleep well last night." I rest my head on your shoulder. "There's a funky tightness right there. Think this walk will help." I move sideways to avoid the sharp edge of a broken seashell. I see our steps behind us preserved in the wet sand above the reach of the outbound tide. I hope they never wash away.

"Do you remember the first time I said I love you?" You speak over the ocean breeze.

"I do, more than sixty years ago. Said the place you took me to for a nightcap scared me. The truth was you frightened me."

Your knowing half smile tells me you understand.

"You promise never to hurt me after hurting me to my core. You will never let anything hurt me again. You take my hand, say you love me. I believe you. Walk right through that door into the rest of our life together."

"Ever regret it?"

"Never," I answer without hesitation.

Your question triggers a no-longer-painful memory. I recall the smell of smoke and alcohol in the noisy dive bar the night you came back to get me. I freeze mid-step in the doorway. I am in love with a man I barely know. Decide to trust you. You could disappear again. Somehow I know you won't.

I remember it all. After a concert in Orlando, bad weather over Texas grounds your plane. You send everyone back to L.A. Claim to hate the music you write and sing. We share a few magical weeks together, and then it all ends. A limo comes; you leave. Not even a goodbye.

I trust my instincts that night in the bar. The best decision of my life. You stay here with me. We build our forever home on the river. Our sons Alex and Jacob grow up there. The world loves your new music. It makes much possible. We have a wonderful life.

"Look at us now, Anthony. So may years later. Our love remains strong. Nothing can separate us." Our eyes meet as a razor-sharp pain pierces my chest like a knife. I crumble to my knees.

"Take my hand again. I love you with all my heart, Sarah." Tears well in your ocean-blue eyes. "This will not hurt you. I will not let it."

Trembling, I reach up, grab your hand. A surge of energy flows up my spine and rushes into my chest. The agony melts away the second our fingers intertwine. I exhale all the air in my lungs. Daylight brightens to brilliant white as my heart beats . . . for the final time.

Sanderlings run in the surf probing the sand for tasty morsels. Gulls glide overhead. There is no sound. The shoreline around me blurs out of focus. We're young again. No longer in my world, I am in yours. As it drifts away, I take one last look around to say farewell to all I love. Hand in hand we turn and run toward the bright light at the end of the beach. I will be next to you forever. Right where I belong.

***

"The key in her pocket opens a convertible in the parking lot way back yonder," the park ranger says to Joe Green, the medical examiner in charge of the scene. "I spoke to her son. Her name is Sarah Whitmore. She's eighty-eight years old. She lives, sorry, lived alone for the last ten years. Oh, the interesting part—she's the widow of the folk singer Tony Whitmore."

"The Tony Whitmore? Wow!" Joe shakes his head as he looks down at the black body bag lying on the stretcher. "I wonder if the media will show up at my office. Let's take her to the morgue." He tries to rub the long day out of his unusually stiff shoulders. "No foul play here; natural causes, mid-step, peaceful, sudden, no pain. The extended arm is odd, like she's reaching for something."

"Getting dark. We need to leave. Can I speak to the person with her today?" The medical examiner scans the small group on the beach. His attention settles on the young couple who discovered her body and reported it.

The young man shrugs. "No one else here when we found her. What makes you think she didn't come alone?"

Joe turns and points at the long trail untouched by the outgoing tide. "Two sets of footprints, side by side. Both stop where she collapsed."

Sherry Mendoza enjoyed her long career at a private university writing policy, compliance guidelines, and audit responses. When she retired, a dear friend urged her to join the Seminole Writer Group. Guided by inspired critiques and patient mentoring she discovered the hard work and pure joy of creative writing.

Kissing Kismet

In college, I'd ridden my department's elevator plenty of times. My mentor's office was located on the fifth floor. By my junior year in 1978, rambling to it was second nature. Nothing indicated that day would be any different.

The elevator opened as usual in the busy first floor corridor. A large maintenance man and I walked on together. After friendly nods, I slipped into automatic. As the elevator rose, my thoughts were wholly about my schedule, a report I had yet to complete, and remembering to get to the store before heading home—barely registering the sizable stranger just feet away.

The elevator door slid open at our landing. He paused for me to disembark, motioning with his hand as if to say, "Ladies first." I rejoined reality to engage him. Since he was closer to the door, I gestured for him to go ahead. I waited until he walked off, then followed, pressing toward my advisor's office, back to completing that shopping list in my head. To my surprise, within steps of the elevator, at first with only the whisper of colossal weight falling, the man collapsed, slamming into the tile floor and flinging me out of my cloud.

Unsure of what just happened beside me, I crept over to him and peered down. "Are, are you okay?" He lay supine and still, the only movement a small stream of blood flowing from the back of his head. He wasn't breathing. Adrenaline began to surge as, in an instant, I was aware that nothing in the world mattered except saving this person. I cried out and shot down the short hall to my professor.

"Larry! Larry!" I banged on his door. "Call an ambulance. NOW! CALL AN AMBULANCE!" I was already racing back when the door opened. "Someone's in trouble!" I yelled behind me.

I didn't have seconds to respond, I had one second. I knew what I needed to do in general but wasn't sure if I remembered individual steps. In lightning speed, I labored to recall practicing with mannequins on the floor of my high school health class. I fell onto my knees close to his face while forcing a review through my mind. NO DISCERNIBLE PULSE FROM HIS NECK. OK, but the steps? HEAD BACK TO OPEN WINDPIPE. HOLD DOWN TONGUE WITH THUMB TO CLEAR

139

THROAT. Racing time, I cocked the man's head back and reached over his face with one hand while simultaneously opening his mouth with the thumb of the other. I shoved my thumb over the back of his tongue to flatten it. CLASP NOSE SHUT. BLOW INTO MOUTH WHILE SEALING IT WITH MINE. I closed off his nostrils, took a deep breath, opened my mouth wide, pressed it around his lips and my thumb, and emptied my lungs. HUGE MAN—BLOW HARDER.

He may have been turning blue by this point, but his dark color and the dim light of the hallway made this impossible to discern. A graduate student in one of the nearby labs heard the commotion and rushed to help. While I forced air into apathetic lungs, the student knelt on the other side of the body and pumped rigorously on the massive chest.

There was no reaction. Without breaking rhythm, I repeated the trials, making my breaths larger if possible, yet the result was the same. I tried again and again, but either he was too big and I too small, or my technique too unpolished, that after several relentless attempts, the man's chest failed to rise and fall.

Although my lips touched his and I held his face, I can't describe how the stranger smelled or how his skin felt. Details evaporated. Social pressures which kept us distant vanished. It seemed immaterial that I was 23 and he perhaps 50. The difference in our gender or skin tone didn't make him more or less sentient. Life and death mattered. I was presented with a critical question of humanity, and even the chance of falling victim to an infection was absurdly inconsequential. The effort to perform vital aid accurately and immediately eclipsed all else, and our difference in body size appeared to be the only problem. Outside of that, nothing was relevant.

A small crowd gathered, and in between mouth-to-mouth contacts I cried out, "He's too big! I'm not helping!" Someone heavier replaced me, but within minutes the paramedics arrived. A legion of professionals worked on the invalid, rapidly assessing, instrumenting and trying to resuscitate him. It didn't take long for them to head to the hospital in a frenzy with the listless body connected to a support system.

From the minute the gentle giant fell, I never again saw a hint of life in him. In all of ten minutes, I witnessed him alive and presumptively well, then comatose and on a respirator. I even attempted to revive him. After the paramedics left, mired in a distant paralysis, I gazed from the foyer as spectators disappeared one by one down hallways and through doors. Left behind while others slid back into routines, I could barely decide on my next move. The adrenaline which flashed through my body in an instant of need subsequently required hours to flush. I didn't know where to go or how to place urgency aside. For the remainder of the day, I aimlessly feigned accomplishing chores.

For an entire week, in fact, it was difficult to shake the trauma. Feelings slowly crystallized out of calamity. That paramedics were at the scene within minutes of calling was consoling. And I felt relief that I didn't suffer medically from the intimate contact. But it was the stranger in the dark gray uniform I could not forget. I sought out other custodians around the building and from them learned his name, although to me he'll always be Kismet. They said he died. I wondered whether or not his family would want to speak with the person who last saw him alive, so I called his home. A young fellow answered, but he was confused about who I was. He tried explaining to others in his room, but no one wanted to come to the phone.

Getting on that elevator, I knew little of this man and hardly noticed him. In an upended moment, though, I wanted to make all the difference in his world, for him. Between the two of us, only I live to remember his final act.

When I think of him, a kaleidoscope of plausible scenes from his life flashes: standing for the first time, playing marbles, blowing birthday candles, watching the Moon landing, enjoying a church picnic, teaching a child to ride a bike, buying his first car, sleeping beside his wife, crying at a funeral, boarding a plane, watching fireworks, resting in the sun, shooting hoops, paying for groceries, repairing a window. Yet, in spite of every chance occasion in his 50-odd years, of every possible stranger with whom he crossed paths, or likely friends or relatives or companions with whom he spent most of his days, the flood of scenes crashes to a halt as our footprints cross when we walk off the elevator together, he and I.

Leah Miller, after almost two decades as a research scientist in both biology and engineering, freelanced as a technical writer for twenty-five years. She now pampers her memoirs that sprouted in the shadows during that time. She spends her free hours in the wilderness.

Yellow Footprints

Yellow footprints glow against the black marble tiles.

Mom warned me I might not be old enough for this sixth-grade trip to D.C., especially this building. "Even though you know our history, there are some pretty scary things in there," she said.

"I want to go," I replied. "I worked hard selling candy to raise the money."

Mom smiled. "You're growing up too fast, Keith."

I thought I was too grown to be afraid.

"Hey, Keith," Michael McKay calls as I follow the footprints into the first exhibit room.

"Hey, Mike."

"This place is a drag," Mike says. "It isn't cool like the Air and Space Museum we saw yesterday."

"Shhh," Someone hisses.

I glance at the yellow footprints. "I need to see it."

Michael groans. "I thought Washington would be fun. Didn't you?"

"I think it's important for everyone to see this." I follow the footprints into a room of glass walls protecting tons of photographs. I put on my glasses to read a few captions.

"They're not even in color," Michael grumbles.

"They're old," I reply.

Michael snorts, "It's impossible."

"What is?"

"Dad says nobody can kill so many people." Michael yawns.

Why doesn't he go? "Read this. A girl tried to save her baby sister." I study the photograph of two young girls in fancy white dresses, ribbons in their hair. "Both were killed."

Even in the dim light, I see Michael's sneer. "They don't look like real people." He hurries to the next room.

Suddenly, the faces are staring at me from every wall. I cannot believe all of them: men, women, children, are dead…murdered. I cannot move.

Michael's voice shatters the spell. "Follow me. I found something cool." He runs off.

I walk, following the yellow footprints.

"You can go inside," Michael says.

I knew the train car was here, but it is still a shock to see it. The footprints vanish at the ramp. I can't see where they start again. "That's okay. I don't want to go in."

Michael yanks me up the ramp. "At least, this is cool."

It is dark. The air is heavy, a musty smell, real, imagined, makes me cough. I reach for the door.

"It's stuck." The heavy wood door will not open.

"Mike, where are you?"

No answer.

A jolt.

Loud clattering sounds, metal against metal. "Are we moving?"

The smell of perspiration wafts up around as sweat-soaked emaciated bodies press against me. The pungent odor makes my stomach churn. The train rattle grows louder. Metal pounds against metal, deafeningly loud. Nowhere to sit. Reeling, unsteady, bodies pressing hard. The train speeds up. "Out! Let me out!" I'm the only one screaming.

I push through the bodies trapping me. No way through. Panic surges. "It's an illusion," I cry. But the motion feels real. I am weak, queasy, about to collapse to the wood planks when the door opens. Yellow footprints at the bottom of the exit ramp are suddenly visible.

I follow the glowing trail. Hold the wall. Catch my breath.

Michael laughs. "Hey, man, I thought I lost you."

"You left." Shaking, I glance back at the cattle car. Harmless. Sad, wide-open, hungry doors. "Let's go."

Michael nearly skips as we follow the footprints. "Hey, Keith, this looks like your bedroom." He laughs again.

A rickety wood table, broken-down cot, and tattered clothes are made to look like they came from a shack in Poland. "My parents came from this town," I say.

"Archie Bunker calls his son-in-law a dumb Polack. Hey, Keith, you always say your parents are from Poland."

I barely hold back from slugging him. "Archie is fiction, to show how prejudice is stupid. Anyone who believes all Polish people are dumb is prejudiced."

Michael answers, but I cannot hear him. There is a loud crash. I reel back as a rifle butt smashes through the rotten wood of the door. Men in black coats and helmets charge in. Screaming, one slams his rifle into a skeletal man rising from the cot. He then aims his demonic red eyes at me.

"Hey, what's wrong with you? You can't sit in here," Michael shouts.

"I got dizzy."

"You're probably hungry," Michael says.

143

Footprints

That could explain it. I follow Michael into a glass tunnel, every inch covered with names engraved into the smoke glass. "My grandparents and Mom's two sisters are somewhere here."

"You'll never find them. There must be a gazillion names," Michael says.

"Six million Jews were killed," I reply, scanning the walls.

"Dad says that's bullshit," Michael says.

"What are you talking about? I lost most of my family during the Holocaust."

"It's phony. Do you really think six million Jews were killed in such a short time? Dad says it was less than one hundred thousand, if any."

"What? It was horrible what Hitler and the Nazis did—"

"My father says they just want people to feel sorry for them," Michael replies.

"It's a fact, you moron! Do you think I made it up?"

"Shhh. Show respect," Someone hisses from the dark.

"I'm sorry," I reply.

"You better be," Michael says. "I'm walking ahead."

"Go on," I say, glad to be rid of him. I see a glow. It almost looks like a candle and then shimmers until a face takes form behind the glass. It is a man, black hair, thin moustache, furrowed forehead, and light blue eyes. "Grandpa? Is it you?"

The man smiles and then the kindly face fades away.

My Grandfather's name is emblazoned in the glass where I saw the face. He was here. I know it. I felt his warmth.

I follow the footprints to the next room. "What's wrong?"

Michael is not moving. He mutters, "Where did they all come from?"

We are in a narrow room, glass on all sides. Behind the transparent walls, there are shoes, countless thousands, packed floor-to-ceiling.

"There are baby shoes," Michael whispers.

Was Michael here all this time?

"What does it mean?" Michael asks.

The room is floor-to-ceiling shoes. Nothing else. I can only stare. It is overwhelming.

"Dad always says it didn't happen," Michael mumbles. "It did. Didn't it?" He searches my face when he says, "Why are there no heels?"

"They tore off the heels and soles to see if anyone hid valuables," I reply.

"These came from the people they killed?"

"Unbelievable, isn't it?"

"So many?" Michael bites his lip and then slowly walks to the exit door. His shoulders tremble.

144

Footprints

I turn back to the shoes. Mom warned me I would see scary things here. Even though I knew the history, My brain cannot accept this room of battered shoes. The heels and soles are missing. Thousands and thousands of ugly shoes. "They're just shoes," I say. When I look for the footprints to escape this room, they are blurred by my tears.

Mark H. Newhouse, born in Germany to Holocaust survivors, is a multi-year RPLA medalist whose novel, The Devil's Bookkeepers, a suspenseful love story set in the Holocaust ghetto his parents survived, won the Gold Medal Historical Fiction and Published Book of the Year in 2019. FWA's Youth Program chairperson and FWA Director, he was last year's Collection Person of Renown.

Admitting D-feet

"Ouch," I said while out shopping at the mall. My pretty shoes pinched me again—another attack by foot soldiers. I decided to take my best friend's advice and cross over. No, not the street like the chicken, nor did I die. I broke down, and my big feet crossed to the other side of the store's first floor, and entered the Nordstrom Men's Shop to try on shoes.

I needed to break out of foot jail. I battled long enough with my huge feet, squashing them into narrow, feminine shoes. I got blisters, corns, and calluses. My feet felt encased in small girdles or gripped by vises. People told me all women had to put up with discomfort; that was our destiny. Centuries ago, Chinese women had their feet bound. Tiny, lotus feet were considered a sign of beauty. These days, a B-width shoe is medium; a C-width is wide. My feet are double-wide like trailers. I'm an average-sized woman, so people appear shocked when I tell them my size. They say, "When they're covered up, you don't look like you have such big ones."

Yes, I wear Ds—like batteries or vitamins. As a child, I walked with my feet pointed outward. When I ran through the sprinklers barefooted, I left wide footprints on the sidewalk. Dad said, "Did a duck run through here?" It was time for a solution.

***

A shoe salesman approached. "Something for your husband?" (I didn't even wear a wedding band.)

I couldn't imagine asking him for feminine shoes, but that's what I wanted. Are there pink, red, or green colored shoes here? I thought. Black, tan, brown, gray, and navy-blue shoes shouted at me from the shelves. I slipped a pair of black loafers on for size and sighed at their comfort. They seemed masculine. My tootsies looked like tugboats pulling me along. I bought the shoes. If I wore slacks and stood, no one would notice my shoes. I might have to stand for the rest of my life.

Feeling confident, I ran to another men's store. The staff chatted to each other about their weekend exploits, ignoring me. I guess they thought I was the wrong gender and not going to buy anything. So, I didn't. I felt like Julia Roberts' character in the movie Pretty Woman where a Rodeo Drive saleswoman shunned and shooed her out due to her revealing and inappropriate attire. Vivian later returned to the store with multiple shopping bags filled with expensive clothing, shook them toward the salesperson, and said, "Big mistake."

A few days later, my stoic and fashion-conscious friend, Geri invited me to lunch. When I sat, my pant legs rode up; she looked down and said, "What kind of shoes are you wearing?"

"Sturdy, comfortable ones," I said. "I need them for a trip up north; it snows there." I squirmed.

"They're clunky and mannish," she said. "How could you wear those in public? You must always put your best foot forward."

My cheeks grew red. My friend, the fashion police, arrested my attention in an hour-long lecture over slender cucumber sandwiches about the positive effects of always looking great when stepping out of the house. I accidently kicked my larger right foot toward her under the table and hit her shin.

***

A shoe salesman once told me I had square feet. "You have short toes, wide width, and high arches. Do you dance?" he said, as he held my left foot.

"Yes," I said. "How did you know?"

"You have dancer's feet."

"I'll have to give them back," I said.

***

Here's another secret dilemma:

> I have two different-sized feet, but no one knows
> Disguised with shoes that have closed toes.

***

I received an invitation to a wedding. I found a shoe store an hour away that carried double-wide dress shoes with adjustable straps in their women's department. Finally. It was worth the time and gasoline expense to step into gold, strappy sandals. The comfortable, lovely shoes prevented me from getting insulted by my fashion-conscious friends. When I saw the reception photos, I noticed no pictures of shoes. Torso to face images prevailed. I could have worn combat boots under my gown, and no one would have known. My two-hundred-dollar gold shoes had a life span of four hours.

After years of fighting the elements (or the elephant-sized feet), I accepted my feet-fate and now wear men's shoes—my step in the right direction. I believe in Bigfoot. It's me. At least I finally admitted D-feet.

Elaine Person teaches writing workshops for libraries and Crealdé School of Art, writes Person-alized poems/stories, and is published in Random House's *A Century of College Humor*, Sandhill Review, FWA Collections, The Florida Writer, The Five-Two, Haikuniverse.com, Poetic Visions, Fresh Fish, and FSPA anthologies. Elaine won Saturday Evening Post's Limerick Contest.

Footprints in the Sand

The scream split the damp air, freezing everyone in place. The farmers, leaning on pickups or sitting on tailgates, looked towards Carl's nearby house. They all started running towards the little house, except Mr. Faircloth, who reached in his truck and pulled out a big flashlight and an equally big pistol.

They found Carl holding Marva, wrapped in a blanket and crying hysterically.

"What the hell is going--?" asked Daddy.

"It was a man -- right there! At – at – th-- the window. He saw me! I didn't have on any clothes, and he saw me!" she said.

"There was a peeking Tom at the window!"

Mr. Faircloth, shining the flashlight on the ground, led them to the bedroom window on the side of the house. "Here's his footprints. He's running towards the highway!"

"There's his footprints," someone said as they trooped across the asphalt. "Ain't seen no car here. He's walking."

"He's going towards the Quarters," said another, motioning, with a wave of his flashlight, in the direction of the dozen or so shacks that was the Negro community.

Bent low, the hunters scoured the damp, sandy lane with flashlights.

"Heahs more footprints -- he's running now!"

"Damn nigger! He's gone --." said someone.

"We gonna lose'im if'n the rain comes back!"

The hunters tracked the footprints to a familiar door in the Quarters: Junior and Nettie Lou's.

"Damn," exclaimed Daddy, speaking for them all. Every man there knew them. Junior was the best tractor mechanic at the John Deere shop. Nettie Lou was our housekeeper and cook.

Daddy and Uncle Bob stepped up on the rickety porch and knocked hard on the door. There was a shuffling noise in the house and then the blinding light as the porch light rushed out onto the brush-broom swept dirt yard, empty except for the footprints. The footprints led straight to the wooden plank door that Nettie Lou had now opened a few inches.

Me and Bill stood in the shadows, listening.

Daddy asked, "Nettie Lou, where's Junior?"

"Junior ain't here Mr. Dubois."

"The hell he ain't." Mr. Faircloth said, "There's his footprints. Open dat damn door!"

They shoved Nettie Lou back from the door and entered the front room. The men knelt and looked at the floor where they saw the footprints outlined in sand. The footprints stopped at the frayed sofa pushed against the wall. They pulled the sofa away from the wall, revealing a pair of work boots with damp sand still stuck to the soles. They charged into the bedroom, where they found Junior, bed covers pulled up to his chin, eyes wide with terror. The covers were thrown back and there was Junior - - - fully clothed.

"Please God, Mr. Dubois!" cried Nettie Lou, "don't let 'em take Junior. He been sick here all day."

There followed the sound of a loud slap and a scream from Nettie Lou as one of the men said, "You lying heifer! We oughta hang you too."

They drug him from the house, tied his hands behind him and threw him in the back of a pickup. The truck drove forward, stopping beneath a huge tree. Two men clambered into the truck, grabbed Junior and pulled him upright. A rope was thrown over a limb and a noose pulled down around Junior's neck. Junior's knees buckled; he would have collapsed if the two men hadn't caught his arms and held him up.

Face turned upward, eyes closed, he prayed for his life. "Please help me Lord," he moaned.

"Please Mr. Faircloth!" cried Nettie Lou. "Don't hang my man. He ain't never gone do dat agin."

"Damn right he ain't," said a man. "We gonna hang dis black bastard."

Nettie Lou lay in the sand, moaning and praying to the Lord for help, saying over and over, "Oh lord help me. Please God. Oh lord help me."

I knew that there were people in those houses listening to the pleading. Listening to the laughter of the mob. But the houses, windows darkened, stood silently.

The headlights of the pickup trucks shone on the small group of men – men who would be in church Sunday morning praising the Lord -- men who were now excited -- leaning, collectively, towards the pickup where Junior, clothes wet with nervous sweat and pee, was shaking and moaning. Voices, anonymous in the darkness, saying, "heist him up slow." "jerk thet rope and see if he can dance." "Put that damn truck in gear and drive on home. He can hang around here tonight."

Laughter at that remark. Lots of laughter. The laughter was growing stronger. The mob bolder. Not as nervous as when the noose had first been placed around Junior's neck. The mob was growing and there was safety in the mob and its anonymity.

A car arrived. Sheriff Rogers got out and began walking towards the truck, speaking loudly "What kind of party have y'all got going here? Y'all barbecuing without calling me?" He was eyeing the crowd as he walked through it. The men stepping back. Making a path for him as he approached the truck.

"I heard y'all was hangin' a nigger. Is he the Peepin' Tom? Y'all better be sure. I don't want no lynching in Pine County tonight. Too damn much trouble nowadays."

"He's the Peepin' Tom. We tracked him right to his bed," said someone from the shadows.

"We fixin' to hang this yere nigger. He was peeking in on Ms. Marva while she wuz bathing," proclaimed a voice from the mob.

"Well -- that ain't no need to hang 'em?" The Sheriff knew most of the men standing in front of him. "I'll take him to my hotel and put him there 'til the judge decides on what to do with him."

"You ain't taking him to no jail. We gonna hang this bastard right here tonight!" said a voice.

The men now shuffled their feet in the damp sand. Scattering their footprints about and waiting for someone, maybe the Sheriff, to decide if there was going to be a lynching. A long silence followed.

Sheriff Rogers was now speaking in a low voice to the mob, hands on his gun belt. His voice carried on the damp spring air. "I just said that there ain't gonna be a lynching. He's going to my jail. Is there anybody here that don't understand that?"

The men removed the noose from Junior's neck, then kicked him, hands and feet still tied, from the back of the truck.

"Goddamn," exclaimed Sheriff Rogers, "he done shit his pants. Y'all put him back in that truck and bring him on to the jail."

Then, they left. A slow procession of taillights on the damp, sandy road towards Hawkins -- only footprints in the sand remained under the giant tree.

***

Saturday morning in the barber shop, the news was all about how Junior had escaped. He had somehow gotten his hands and feet freed from the rope that bound him and had jumped from the truck as they were crossing the Altamma Bridge.

***

Like others, Junior was never seen nor heard from again.

Jim Ramage lives in Yulee, Florida, when he is not working or traveling in off-the-beaten-path locations.

Our Living Testament

Monday
Ran into Saturday
In a wink
And I had little
Time to think?
Life flashed by
Comet-like, as if
Stealing days
From my life's
Last season.

I glance back
At long stretched
Past and see a track
With two pairs
Of footprints,
Yours very close
To mine, a living
Testament of love
Defined, for our
Children and
Grandchildren,
Our landmarks etched
With golden memories
That they some day
may find.

Monday turned to Saturday
In a wink, time to stop
And think! Sunday is here.
Must hold each moment dear
In these our final years.
Time to make more footprints. Together.

Amarilys Gacio Rassler is the author of the book, *Cuban-American, Dancing On The Hyphen,* used by Oregon State University for cultural studies. She is an award-winning author of fiction and nonfiction, prose and poetry. She is currently working on her memoir, *Beyond the Veil, Encountering Demons.*

Letting Go

I flipped through the next book on the pile and shook it by the spine for good measure.

Going through my eccentric mom's things proved to be a painstaking process. An expert at hiding keepsakes, she preferred tiny nooks and crannies to jewelry boxes. I knew to go through every pocket and old purse searching for secret treasures. I doubted she'd squirrel anything away in a book, but I didn't want to miss something important.

Since Dad left when I was ten, Mom had been more careful with household details, so I knew that given the time she would've put her belongings in order and left itemized to-do lists. But a brief illness took her at only fifty-four, leaving me, shell-shocked, to navigate my own way through her possessions.

Aunt Jess and I didn't need to draw straws to see who would declutter Mom's bedroom, with its jam-packed book nook. As a recently-converted minimalist, Aunt Jess preached tossing. She lectured me on clutter, rolled her eyes at her best friend's gnome collection, and took pride in having only three decorative pieces in her living room. To me the room looked like an airplane hangar, empty and lifeless, but she considered the space a beautiful incarnation of her inner soul.

Mom's cozy suburban home packed with a lifetime's accumulation brought a crazed look to Aunt Jess's eyes. Still, she agreed to work on the easy places like the laundry room and the kitchen. It's not hard to toss expired oatmeal.

I gave the next book a shake and picked up two more.

My aunt poked her head around the door jamb, a wisp of graying hair fluttering. "Lindsey, how about we go out for lunch?"

"Sounds good." Prepared to add both books to the 'give away' pile, I shook one in each hand.

"Come on. I want to beat the lunch rush." Aunt Jess hurried away.

A small card floated down from one of the books.

Two tiny inked footprints, announcing a baby's arrival, were centered on a square of cardstock rimmed in faded blue. I brought the card close enough to read the cursive name: Clinton Ross. A prickling sensation traveled down my neck.

According to the date on the front, a baby boy sharing my mother's maiden name, had been born four years before me. The back of the card was blank. I stayed frozen as my mind clicked through suppositions, none of them good.

Racing through the house, I caught up to my aunt. "Did you know about this?" I thrust out the card. "Mom had another baby?" My voice sounded stiff and squeaky.

Aunt Jess squinted, her forehead puckering. "Oh, honey," she whispered.

I took a step back from her outstretched arms. She'd known. "No." I held up a hand. Mom and Aunt Jess both lied to me. I had to get out, get away. I needed fresh air. I darted outside, not caring where I went.

Everything felt jumbled and confused. I had a brother. That meant I wasn't an only child. Had Dad known? I strode along the winding tree-shaded sidewalk, a breeze rustling nearby palm fronds. Wait. Was Dad the father? Who was? Did it matter? I'd always wanted a brother, but not this way. By the time I reached the next street, I was close to hyperventilating.

Aunt Jess caught up on a rusty bicycle. "Lindsey, we were going to tell you last month."

What was she talking about? A month ago, Mom was too sick to speak. "Who's we?" I slowed.

"Remember Crystal was so excited about doing her DNA?"

I stopped, and my aunt quit peddling, straddling the bike. My cousin had chattered nonstop about the DNA test she'd gotten last Christmas, but after weeks of making absurd guesses about her ethnicity, she'd grown quiet. In hindsight, Crystal's sudden silence was uncharacteristic.

I whispered, "She found him. He's alive."

Aunt Jess lay the bike down and took a tentative step. "He contacted her when their DNA matched. They've been texting."

I shook my head. "Why didn't Mom say anything? She should have told me." My words sounded accusing and came out harsher than I intended.

Aunt Jess came closer. "I think she wanted to forget." She looked down.

A car sped past, music blaring, jolting my thoughts. I tried to come up with my next question, wishing I could ask Mom instead.

Before I spoke, Aunt Jess continued, "She was in college, and Grandma and Grandpa didn't approve."

I lifted my head. "Imagine that."

"You have no idea. They were even worse back then. Their pride and joy had disgraced them." Her shoulders quivered, and she seemed fragile and diminished.

In that moment she reminded me of Mom, and I realized they were both a lot like me. Sensitive, driven, a little stubborn. But what was young Mom like? She must have been terrified to face her parents. I knew without being told that ending the pregnancy would not have been an option, which left giving the baby up. How sad she never had a choice.

Aunt Jess reached for my hand. "He's had a good life," she said, maybe trying to convince herself. "Your mom would have wanted to meet him. By the time he found Crystal, she wasn't well enough." My aunt swallowed, blinking, before clasping my other hand. "You have to understand. The reason she didn't tell you had nothing to do with you. It was her. She had too much . . ." Aunt Jess scanned the tree-lined street. "baggage. I think she always meant to explain. She ran out of time."

I sighed, unsure what to say.

"You have choices," she went on. "You don't need to hold this against her. Or Grandma and Grandpa. Let go of that old junk." She dropped my hands to gesticulate. "Clear things out." She paused, tipping her head toward the sun. "That way, you'll have room for something new."

I tilted my chin skyward, too, letting the breeze ruffle my hair. Maybe she was right. Mom was gone. I could stay angry, but why? None of this was Clinton's fault either.

"You're right. I should let stuff go. Thanks," I turned to walk back toward Mom's, pausing for Aunt Jess to pick up the rickety bike and follow.

"Want to meet him? He goes by Cliff now, Cliff Belmond."

I gave an assured nod. "I always wanted a big brother. And I've already got a present for him."

"You do?" She raised an eyebrow.

"The card Mom saved with his footprints."

Lines crinkled around my aunt's dusky blue eyes. "I'm sorry we didn't tell you. I'm sorry you found out this way. But, I'm glad you know. Secrets keep us apart." She put the bike's kickstand down as we reached my mother's yard. "Giving the card away is a nice gesture, and opening your heart is even better."

I stepped close to hug Aunt Jess. "I'm glad you were here to help."

"I'm always here for you." She squeezed me tight. We stayed that way for a long time before she released me. "But maybe we can put this bike in the junk pile?"

I laughed, nodding. "Absolutely."

Cathy Rebhun, prize-winning author of short fiction and memoir pieces, has been published by Reader's Digest, the Florida Writer's Association, and Odet Literary Journal. She belongs to a writing critique group and lives in Hillsborough County.

Turtles Come Home

"Cara! Get the hell out of there."

"Sonny, come look at these marks in the sand. What could have made them?"

"Didn't you read the sign?"

"What sign?"

"This beach is a preserve for turtles. Like, who gives a shit? The turtles come back to this beach every year to lay their eggs. Hey, I wonder what turtle eggs taste like. I'm hungry."

"Don't you dare. Look over there. A turtle is digging a hole. There are mounds all over. It's awesome that they come back home to have their babies."

"Turtles are only good cooked in a pot. Come out of there and make me some breakfast. NOW!"

Sonny headed off down the beach toward Tent City at the other end of the lagoon. His tall, muscular frame carried him easily over the shifting sand. He didn't need to look back. He knew she would follow.

Cara looked again at the turtles and realized the marks in the sand were turtle footprints from the water's edge to the mounds and back to the water. "Turtles, you inspire me."

She stepped over the low barrier of rocks and headed down the beach at a run. Her petite body, packed with muscle from lifeguarding in her teens, didn't take long to catch Sonny.

Together they entered the edge of Tent City, a closely built network of fifty or so small tents, organized in groups of ten around a fire-pit. When they reached their tent, Sonny grabbed his guitar and settled on a log next to several other men with instruments from their group.

The men ran the camp and the women were expected to do their bidding. Cara proceeded to a large box trunk where foodstuffs were kept for use by the group.

Lucy joined her from the adjacent tent. "Can I help?"

"Appreciate that, Lucy. We'll need hot water for oatmeal. I'll set up the rest."

Lucy returned from heating water over the fire-pit and mixed in the oatmeal. They delivered the filled bowls to the four men sitting around the pit practicing for their evening gig. The income from local gigs paid for food, incidentals, and liquid libation, meaning beer, not necessarily in that order.

"Cara! What is this shit?" Sonny screamed.

"I'm sorry, Sonny. It's all we have," Cara said, expecting a nasty verbal or physical retort. He glared at her and grumbled.

"Let's go for a walk down the beach," Lucy said.

"Great idea. I want to show you the turtles laying their eggs," Cara said.

When they got to the preserve, Lucy blurted out, "I'm pregnant."

"What!" Cara said. "Are you sure? I thought Rick didn't want…"

"He doesn't. But a couple months ago, when the guys all got drunk, he didn't use protection. I'm really scared, Cara." Tears streamed down Lucy's face. She wiped them away with her hands. "If he finds out, he'll kill me."

"Rick could change his mind."

"No way. His threats are real. I don't dare tell him. What am I going to do?"

Cara nodded towards the turtles on the other side of the low rock wall. "See the turtles coming ashore. They come back to the place they were born to lay their eggs. It's a sign. Do what the turtles do. Go home and raise your baby."

"I haven't talked to my parents for a year. I'm not sure they will take me back, especially with me pregnant." Lucy wiped away fresh tears.

"They'll take you back. Mothers love their children no matter what."

"Oh, but you didn't see the scene I made when I left home. Rick was such a charmer in those days."

"You need to call your parents."

"Exactly how in hell do I do that? Rick won't allow me to use his phone and I have no money."

"Simple. Offer to go buy more beer. I've done it before. They'll all chip in money for that. You'll have enough to call your parents. Let's go."

***

Lucy's offer to restock the beer supply was met with applause. Lucy and Cara took off to town with a pull-cart for the beer, and more than enough money.

"You make your call and I'll get the beer." Cara headed for the counter.

Cara was putting the beer in the cart when a man wearing a Coast Guard uniform entered the store. She quickly scribbled a note on her receipt and handed it to the man. He read it and looked up at her pleading face, then nodded.

Cara left the store in good spirits and met Lucy running toward her, shouting excitedly, "They want me to come home! Dad's coming to get me tomorrow. Oh, Cara! I'm so happy."

"He's not coming to Tent City is he? That could be a disaster. The men don't like to lose their bitches."

"Yes, I know that for sure. Dad's meeting me in town. You're to come with us."

"Go with you? That's very kind, but I can't do that."

"Sure you can. I know how Sonny treats you. You need to leave too."

"Yes, I know. You see, that drunken night you mentioned is responsible for more than your baby. Sonny would be worse than Rick if he found out."

"Oh, no! All the more reason to come with me."

"When I leave, Sonny has to believe I died or he will hunt me down. I must cut all ties for good."

"Do you have a plan?"

"I'm going to follow the turtles. Sonny doesn't know I'm a strong swimmer. The Coast Guard should be waiting for me."

"Brilliant!" Lucy said, "We better not look too happy or the men will be suspicious."

***

The camp came alive before dawn next morning with chatter about the Coast Guard buzzing the coastline, which they did some times to check out Tent City.

Suddenly, Sonny came storming out of his tent, "Where's Cara? I bet she's with those damn turtles. She'll get herself in trouble."

Lucy peeked out of her tent and listened to the ruckus. Cara's missing? This is it! She, and many from camp, followed Sonny as he stormed down the beach to the turtle preserve.

When they reached the low wall, Sonny fell to his knees and pulled free Cara's scarf caught in the rocks. He looked over the wall and began moaning.

On the other side of the low stonewall were human footprints. They trailed along the water's edge, overlapping the turtle prints, and disappeared into the waves.

***

Cara was nearing the Coast Guard boat when she stopped swimming and looked back. From her distance, she could just make out lights in the camp and people walking on the beach. She planned her escape well, she thought. It didn't occur to her that the large traffic of turtles draw sharks.

 **Carolee Russell**, a member of FWA, WLOV and W4Kids, has written, Illustrated, and published *Murder in the Haunted House* (Hoffer Award winner), *A Wish For Algie*, *In His Time*. She illustrated *SuperBudz, Crystal Discovers The Glow, Poems for the Funnybone*. She's currently working on *A Race To Murder* and *Summer Vacation*.

Beyond the Field

She turned to retrieve the shoe in the dirt behind her. The hand me downs were too big, especially as the laces had long since disappeared. She shoved her thin foot back into the shoe, picked up her digging tool and stared at the row ahead.

"Irina. The potatoes. Stop daydreaming and dig the potatoes. The oven waits." Her mother, working in a nearby row wiped her face with the szmata she kept tucked in a pocket of her skirt.

Obedient to the quiet reminder, Irina resumed her labor, dragging the burlap potato sack behind her. Most of the women workers had hoes to dig with, but today Irina was given one with a short broken handle, forcing her to uproot the potatoes on her hands and knees.

A soft warm rain started to fall. She welcomed the feel of it on her back, and the trickle through her hair. She pretended it was water from the bathroom shower and clearly pictured the small octagon black and white tiles of the bathroom in their home. Mama had kept it so clean. Irina imagined she smelled the lemon scented soap her mother had used for scrubbing.

A hint of sun shone through the rain to further brighten the moment...then a corner of her makeshift tool pierced a rotting potato, and the illusion vanished.

To overcome the tedium of her labor and distract from the ache in her shoulders, Irina tried to recall various lessons from her school in Krakow. She wondered where her classmates were now. It had been over a year since she had last seen them.

The rain subsided, and she heard footsteps approaching from behind. Out of the corner of her eye, she saw the high black mudded boots as he stalked by her. She didn't look up. She knew who he was. When he was at a safe distance away, she leaned over to spit in his footprint. Even at twelve years old, she knew about the oven.

Joan O. Scharf, a native of the Catskill Mountain area of New York State, adventured from coast to coast and Europe before discovering the beauty of Florida. Her flash fiction and short stories appear in several magazines and anthologies. She has written three books, and co-authored a fourth.

Farrier's Footprints

Rob Nichols squinted through the pickup's windshield at the April sun rising in the sky over Odessa. "Gonna be a hot one today," he said and glanced at his sullen, nine-year-old stepson in the passenger seat. Logan hadn't said a word since leaving the house before daybreak.

He backed the farrier trailer to the barn entrance. "First stop." Rob shut off the engine and checked the list of horses he would be doing at the barn. "We have two horses to trim and one that needs shoeing. Remember what I said about being careful around the horses?" When the boy did not reply, Rob took a deep breath. "Your mom told me you have a school questionnaire to fill out."

"I still don't know why I couldn't go with Mom," Logan said.

"Your mother thought you should learn about my job. You spent Take Your Child to Work Day with her for the past two years." Rob wondered if Logan following him around today could possibly improve their relationship like Mandy expected.

With a sigh, Logan pulled a folded paper from his pocket. He spread it against his leg and flattened the creases. "What's your job?"

"I'm a farrier, third generation." Rob remembered riding with his father when he was about Logan's age and asking dozens of questions. He had followed his father's footprints into the horseshoeing business, like his father before him. However, Rob had married late in life, Mandy didn't want any more kids, and Logan hadn't shown any interest in his profession. The family business would end with Rob.

Logan's pencil hovered over his paper. "How do you spell farrier?"

"It's on the side of the trailer." Rob opened the truck door and stepped out. "Let's go."

"Nichols and Son, Farriers" in bold black letters covered the side of the trailer. After Logan wrote the answer to the first question on his paper, Rob lifted the side door to expose his workspace and tools.

The boy gasped. "What's all this stuff?"

With a chuckle, Rob pulled out his leather apron and fastened it around his waist. "These are the things I use when shoeing or trimming a horse."

He pointed out the drill press, grinder, anvil, and forge. Then, he placed the hoof knife in his apron pocket.

A petite, white-haired woman hurried down the barn aisle. "I'm so glad you're here. Bonnie and I went on a trail ride yesterday and now she's limping."

"Let's take a look at her," Rob said. He gestured for Logan to step forward. "Miss Sue, this is Logan. He's learning about horseshoeing today."

The woman smiled at Logan. "You're learning from the best. Your dad always takes such good care of the horses here."

"He's not my dad," Logan said and crossed his arms.

Rob quickly added, "Logan is my stepson."

Sue waved a fly away from her face. "It's nice you're getting to spend the day together."

Rob nodded, but he doubted the day would go well. Logan's tight lips and narrowed eyes reflected the boy's attitude.

They followed the woman halfway down the wide barn aisle to a stall. The wooden nameplate across the front proclaimed "My Bonnie Lass" in bright red letters. A large gray horse poked her head over the stall door and whinnied.

As the woman led the mare out of the stall, Rob watched the horse's hesitant steps. "She's favoring the right front. Logan, see how she lifts her head when she puts that foot down?"

At the boy's puzzled expression, Rob explained, "Horses can't tell us what's wrong, so we watch their body language for clues."

Bending down, Rob lifted the horse's front foot. After examining the sole, he rose and patted the mare's shoulder. Then, he rubbed the stiffness in his lower back. "Looks like a stone bruise."

"Poor dear. It must have happened when we rode over some rocky patches yesterday," Sue said.

"Give her a week of rest, Miss Sue. She should be fine after that. If not, let me know and I'll check for an abscess."

When Bonnie was back in her stall, Rob set to work on the horses scheduled for a trim. From across the barn aisle, he watched Logan approach Bonnie until the horse curled her upper lip.

Logan backed away quickly. "She tried to bite me."

"No, she's smelling that orange you had for breakfast." Rob frowned. The boy's afraid of horses. "Let her smell you."

From under the belly of a bay gelding, he watched Logan inch toward Bonnie and tentatively touch her whiskered muzzle. Good boy, face your fears. "Logan, what other questions you got there?"

With a rustle of paper, Logan read aloud, "What training do you need for your job?"

"I learned from my father, and he learned from his father. I was about your age when I started helping."

Logan came closer. "What did you do?"

Rob laughed at the memory. "I pushed a broom. See all these trimmings on the ground? They'll need to be swept up."

The paper rustled again. "What is your favorite part of the job?"

Slowly, Rob straightened up, stretching his back. "Problem-solving. Yes, definitely problem-solving. Like what we did with Bonnie. You heard how happy Miss Sue was to have an answer to Bonnie's problem."

Logan wrote the answer on his questionnaire. "What's your least favorite part of the job?"

Rob inhaled slowly. "You promise not to tell your mom?"

The boy's eyes widened and he stepped nearer.

"This has got to be our secret." Rob waited for Logan to nod. "Getting kicked by a horse. It doesn't happen often, but it does happen. I don't want your mom worrying. You understand?"

Logan smiled. "She does worry about things."

It was the first smile Rob had gotten from the boy. "Maybe you should write that my least favorite part is getting dirty. She'll agree with that too." He held his filthy, calloused hands open for Logan to see. "Wait till you see how dirty you are at the end of the day."

They both laughed. Rob slapped the gelding on the rump, and a cloud of dust swirled into the air.

Two horses later, Rob put his rasp back in the trailer and took his apron off.

A slight breeze ruffled the paper in Logan's hand. "Last question. What career advice would you give me?"

Rob rubbed his hands against his jeans and thought about all the wisdom his father had shared. "Be the best you can be at whatever you decide to do."

Logan scribbled the words onto his paper. "All done."

"Not exactly," Rob said. "There's a broom on the trailer. You can sweep up." He pointed at the hoof trimmings on the ground.

For a minute, the two faced each other. Their eyes locked together.

Logan folded his paper and put it in his pocket. "Does this mean you're going to teach me to be a farrier?"

Rob's heart beat faster. "If you want to learn, I'll teach you." Maybe Nichols and Son would continue; another generation might follow in the farrier's footprints.

K. L. Small is originally from New York City, and now lives in Brooksville, FL, with her husband, on a horse ranch called Carousel Acres, which they share with three horses (Rory, ShyAnne, Skylark), three cats (Rose, Dorothy, Blanche), and assorted wildlife.

Footprints

"Jess . . . JESS!" Roy called, treading water. He spun in a circle, searching for any sign of her. He shouted again. Nothing. Panic rose in his throat. He didn't know if he could make it to the bottom. He called again and, finally, she answered.

"I'm here . . . ugh . . . I'm . . . here!" Jess called, sputtering canal water.

"Oh, thank goodness. Swim to the bank."

Jess kicked hard to stay afloat. The billowing bell bottoms of her jeans brushed against her ankles. It was unnerving.

"Do you think there are any alligators in here?" she asked, knowing the answer but hoping Roy would lie to her.

"No. The impact would have scared them away," he said. That's why she loved him.

They paddled along the bank searching for a gentle slope to climb. Roy hoisted himself out, then offered his young lover a dripping hand. She took it, praying an alligator wouldn't gnash at her feet before she could escape.

They climbed the steep bank, avoiding broken beer bottles and fire ant piles that dotted their path. Stopping on the slope to catch their breath, they gazed into the murky water. Under the surface, the old Mercury was dying – exhaling its last breath. Bubbles rushed to the top and disappeared; the car's fading footprint.

"Hey, you all right?" he asked.

She turned her head to look at him. "I think so . . . my head hurts a little."

"You bumped it on the roof when we hit the water. You were down there a long time. You scared me, Jess!"

"I . . . I think I was dazed. It's all like a dream. Oh, Roy! Your car!"

Roy hung his head. "Yeah. My dad's going to kill me. He loved that old car." He thought for a moment and said, "Listen, it would make matters worse if they knew we were skipping. We'll say this happened after school, okay?"

"Sure," she said. "Roy, my purse is down there. So are my sandals."

He wrapped an arm around her and kissed the top of her head. "I'm sorry," he murmured.

"Yeah, well, maybe next time you decide to do fishtails, don't do it on a canal road, okay?" She pulled away to squeeze water from her hair, then combed her fingers through it.

"I don't understand. I've done a hundred fishtails on this road." He drew in a sudden breath. "The cement!' he said. "There were four bags in the trunk. It threw off the balance. That's why we went in. God dammit." He picked up a rock and hurled it across the canal. It landed on the opposite bank with a thunk, then rolled into the water. He threw another, then another.

Jess watched the last bubbles trickle to the top and break through the iridescent film spreading over the water. She said softly, "We're lucky the windows were down."

They grew quiet, listening to the sounds around them. Cicadas buzzed in the trees. A catfish surfaced for a gulp of air. Somewhere, a single engine plane droned in the sky.

When it was time to go they hauled themselves to the top of the embankment. The sun beat mercilessly upon them now. Jess stepped gingerly onto the road.

"Ouch!" she said, bending to extract a broken shell from between her toes.

"You can't walk on the road like that." Roy kicked off his sneakers. "Take them," he said.

She hesitated. The thought of him walking over the sharp pebbles in his socks bothered her. She said, "I have an idea. We'll each wear a sock and a shoe. If our feet get sore, we'll switch." If nothing else, Jess was pragmatic.

Roy removed a tube sock. She wrung it out and slipped it on, doubling it over the sole of her foot.

"How far to the main road?" she asked, sliding her other foot into the swampy shoe and tightening the laces. She walked a few steps and deemed it bearable.

"Pretty far, I guess. Five or six miles."

Jess couldn't picture the distance and asked, "How far is that from my house? As far as Winn-Dixie?"

"Further," he said. "More like to the shopping plaza on the highway."

"Oh, wow," she said. She and Lisa sometimes walked to the Zayre department store, but always with stops for ice cream or fountain drinks along the way.

They walked past a grackle perched on a telephone pole. It took flight, complaining loudly as it went. Roy brushed a forearm across his brow. Jess glanced over her shoulder and smiled at the unusual tracks they were leaving in the dust.

He looked sidelong at her. "You're lucky you're wearing a bra," he said, "I can see right through your blouse."

"You would've had an eyeful if we'd made it to the Steel Bridge," she teased. She stopped walking and turned to look back.

"What's wrong?" Roy said.

"I just remembered . . . my grandmother's silver dollar. It's in my wallet. It's all I had to remember her by. Oh, and the perfume you gave me for my birthday. And, oh my God, my house key! How am I going to explain this to my mother? Shit. I am so grounded." She sighed and tears welled in her eyes. "We might as well say goodbye for a month."

Roy felt awful. "Listen," he said, pulling her to him. "It's going to be all right. I'll get Bill to dive down with his scuba gear and get your purse. I know exactly where the car is. There's a little mango tree across from where we went in. Funny, huh? A mango tree growing in the middle of nowhere."

It was a mystery. Like a single footprint in the sand, Jess thought.

Roy went on. "I'll talk to your mom. I'll tell her it was my fault. She'll understand. She's crazy about me."

Jess was dubious. "I lost a key once when I was nine. She smacked me in the face . . . hard."

"She won't smack me. If she does, I'll smack her back. Bap bap bap!" He cut the air with his hand and she laughed.

"Baby, have I ever told you you're my hero?"

"About a million times. Hey, look! There's a truck coming. Aw, don't look so worried. I'll see if he can give us a lift into town." He waved an arm and the truck slowed.

"Oh, Roy, I wish you wouldn't. What if he's dangerous? What if he's a serial killer? Oh, please don't!"

"It'll be fine, babe. There are no serial killers in Homestead."

"How do you know that?"

"Well, if there was, we would've heard about him by now. – Hey, man. My car just went in the canal back there. Can we catch a ride with you?"

The driver nodded. Roy and Jess hopped into the bed of the pickup and disappeared down the road.

A few hours later, an old farmer walking his dog wondered where the strange footprints had gone.

D.J. Snyder grew up in a military family, settling in Florida in 1976. She recently decided to try her hand at short-story writing and draws inspiration from her childhood experiences. D. J. lives with her husband in a quiet equestrian community in South Florida.

Leave No Trace

Tall pines swayed in the breeze as we crested the top of a 50-ft Florida mountain. My son and daughter ran in front of me, gloating at the success of climbing a hill they refer to as "Summit Mountain."

In my children's defense, they were born and raised in this flat state. They're not used to the elevation. But as we sat on a downed pine log and my husband shared a bag of jelly beans, I took a moment to appreciate their enthusiasm. We'd walked five miles through pine forests and an oak hammock with little change in scenery. When hiking in Florida, it's important to celebrate the small things.

After our snack, we adjusted our hydration packs and made the short trek down the sandy slope to the bottom. The kids continued ahead, scouting pinecones to hit with their walking sticks.

It wasn't always this easy hiking as a family. When my husband and I decided to spend more time outdoors, the kids were averse to the idea. Our first few hikes carried a soundtrack of complaints and whining, and not just from the kids.

Their comments revolved around the distance and time they spent walking. As for me, well, I complained about not having enough food. One of the most valuable lessons we'd learned was to keep our blood sugar levels up. Now we always pack candy on our adventures. By that January afternoon, we'd grown accustomed to the routine. And the jelly beans.

The pandemic of 2020 caused the cancellation of all our activities. We had to find something to do as a family that didn't involve staring at a screen all day and allowed us to stay away from others. Naturally, that led us outdoors.

On our first hike, I took a picture of a sign at a trailhead that read, Take nothing but pictures. Leave nothing but footprints. The sign served as a reminder to tread lightly on the land, to leave no trace.

As more of us seek solace from society in nature, it's important to follow the Leave No Trace principle. This principle states that we are to leave nature as we found it. Anything we bring in comes out. Anything we find stays in nature where it belongs. I had an opportunity to teach this principle to my kids during our first hike back in July.

My daughter is an avid collector of everything, and the forest is full of treasures. When we first began our long day hikes, she asked if she could keep some of the tiny pinecones that dotted the forest floor. It became a great teaching moment for my kids.

I explained to them that those pinecones, and everything else in the forest, belong to the forest. If we want these natural places to be around when they're older, we need to leave them as they are.

This doesn't translate to something kids understand. So, I made my next point on their level. I said, "This is where the animals live. It's their home. Would you like it if someone took your things from our home?"

They said they wouldn't, of course. When they're older, we'll discuss the importance of balanced ecosystems. But for the time being, I got my point across.

My son has taken the Leave No Trace principle to heart, even picking up the jelly beans he's dropped in the sand and eating them anyway. I'd like to believe it's because he truly cares about the environment.

One pleasant afternoon in October, we tried a new trail further from the house. Our inability to read the map led us down a forest service road for a mile before we turned around and found the trailhead we were looking for.

This brings me to another thing nature has taught us, navigation. We've learned to rely on technology to do everything for us. Though my husband and I pride ourselves on our ability to do things like navigating without a GPS, this isn't the first time we've gotten lost.

I learned to appreciate mistakes like these, for the lessons they'd taught us. We explained to the kids what they need to do if they get lost, what not to do, and how to stay calm. As for my husband and me, well, these mistakes have taught us to be patient and appreciate our time outdoors, even if it doesn't go to plan.

We backtracked down the service road, which showed heavy use by campers and hunters. About every thirty yards or so, we stumbled across empty glass bottles, beer cans, energy drink cans, and beef jerky wrappers. It showed us a distinct difference between this path and the pristine places we'd grown used to. Not everyone who goes into nature follows the Leave No Trace principle.

***

This January afternoon the temperature is in the upper 60s and the sun is shining. It's the kind of day we pray for all summer.

Out here in the woods, we're away from the stresses of twenty-four-hour news, social media, and screens. We can't hear the constant buzz of household appliances, the ping of a message on our phones, or the neighbor's dogs. It's quiet, calm, and beautiful.

Across the orange and red landscape of recently burned pine forest, we spotted three white-tailed deer bounding through the blackened trees. A red-shouldered hawk cried overhead, and we stopped for a moment to watch it. I love these moments with my family.

During our two-hour walk, there wasn't a single complaint. My daughter hadn't asked for TV time. My son didn't mention a video game once. I've noticed my kids don't fight when we go hiking. They seem to become more content the further they get from the sensory overload that engulfs their typical day.

I take in a long, slow breath to savor the moment. When I look up at the clear blue sky, a small insight creeps into my mind. Maybe if we all spent more time in nature enjoying the little moments, we might be better off. This insight is neither profound nor new. And yet, we seem to forget that even during the most hectic of times, nature is still there for us, providing solace from the stresses of daily life.

When we step onto the gravel parking area at the end of our hike, I think about the sign again. Take nothing but pictures. Leave nothing but footprints. Over the last few months, we've taken more than pictures from the trails. We've taken memories.

I turned back to see the footprints we'd left behind. But we already lost them to the soft sands of the trail.

E.M. St. Pierre is a member of the Sounding Board critique group in Tampa. She is currently querying a middle-grade adventure novel while working on other projects. When she's not writing, Erin enjoys hiking, yoga, rock climbing, and spending time with her husband and kids in the sunshine.

A One-Legged Seagull
My Story

In the surf, I went to play.
It was an ordinary day.
Just then a wave began to swell
I tried to run but then I fell.

A tangled ball of fishing line
snagged around that foot of mine.
I gave a pull. I gave a tug,
but all that did was make it snug.

No way out that I could see.
I could not get my left foot free.
My leg was hurt. I squawked a cry.
A man was fishing quite nearby.

"I'm sorry if my carelessness
got you in this tangled mess.
I will not leave you in the sand."
He picked me up in one strong hand.

He took me to the bird rescue;
for there was something they could do.
At times I felt so very sad,
and sometimes I felt very mad.

I had to practice every day
to get around a different way.
Now I can hop and I can fly.
I've found my way back to the sky.

Footprints

When I fly and then I land
I leave one footprint in the sand.
Yes, I lost my foot that day;
but here I am and I'm okay!

Mary J. Staller, an FWA member and cofounder of the FL Gulf Coast Writers Circle, has published short stories and a children's rhyming picture book. She finds great inspiration at the beach.

Extant

From an early age, I've tugged and pulled at the Gordian Knot of life's meaning and its finality.

As a young boy, I spent summers on a remote lake in the Blue Ridge mountains. Life presented itself as fragile inside the wood shingle cottage cocooned in old-growth forest.

My mom and dad were out for the evening. I sat on the front porch and watched the sun drop into the tall oaks. Orange spots too bright to look at for very long danced among the breaks in their branches.

After sunset, I turned on the front light for my parents and went up to bed in the second-story loft under the high A-frame. I pushed open the wavy glass window and turned on my reading lamp. I was nice and toasty tucked into my cotton quilt.

A gust blew up from the lake and brushed oak limbs against the roof. I heard a howl deep in the woods. The trees moaned and creaked.

My window banged against the wood frame. Lightning flashed. The lights went out. I could not see my hands, even held close to my eyes. I sucked in deep breaths. For the first time, I faced fear.

I groped in the dark along rough plaster before arriving at the window. I heard the howling again. It sounded closer. The window banged harder.

I heard stories of ravenous wolves lurking in the forest. Could wolves climb trees?

The window slapped open, then banged shut. I had to close it. Had to keep out all the bad things. I grabbed for the handle. The glass smashed. I grimaced in pain. My fist was wet and sticky with blood.

I crawled back to bed and pulled the covers over my head. The howling and branches crashing against the roof kept me from closing my eyes. Was the wolf nearby? Was I going to die?

***

Science offered well-ordered recipes for analyzing and dissecting my undergraduate world. The equations and recitations came easy. My professors rewarded me with accolades and top honors.

Philosophy was the monkey wrench in my march to order the world.

Leibniz had me observing clocks scattered across the universe to ensure they all displayed the same time. Aristotle demanded I prove time couldn't exist unless something moved from here to there.

Worst of all, there was the Greek philosopher, Zeno—and his paradox. I could imagine him calling to me, "You can never reach your goal."

I, at that time, could clearly see where I was going—and therefore, I could reach my goal!

Zeno challenged me. "Take a one-mile walk."

I said, "Sure."

Zeno asked me, "After you've gone a half-mile, how much is left for you to travel—and reach your goal?"

I retorted, "That's easy. One-half mile." Was this guy stupid?

Then he snuck up on me with this one, "I want you to travel half the remaining distance. What is the distance that remains?"

I gave that some thought and answered, "Half of what remains—one-fourth of a mile."

He then told me to travel half the remaining distance. He asked, "How much remains?"

At this point, I was feeling played. I had to answer, "Half of what remains. Which is one-eighth of a mile."

Right away, he shot back with, "How much is left to travel?"

I said, "Half the remaining distance which is…"

Zeno laughed cruelly and said, "We can play this game forever. You will always have one-half of the distance remaining."

He smiled down on me like the fool I was. "You cannot prove to me you will ever reach your goal."

Zeno was my nemesis. I had no clue he would someday offer me hope of eternal life. I was too young to care.

***

It was my fortieth birthday. I sidestepped the pale yellow and orange poppies of early spring that pushed their way through the cracked sidewalk of San Francisco's Sunset district.

I mounted the uneven steps of a Spanish mission that had traded its sanctuary lamp for the diverse spiritual offerings promised to the lost souls of Haight Ashbury.

Two enormous lilac bushes framed the misbegotten church's whitewashed doors. I was here to expand my spirit and the wafts of sweet almond and green leaves did their job. As I entered, a deep breath surprised me with the tiny white flowers' haunting essence of decay.

On this last day of Spirituality Search, I sat on a creaky chair with my sandaled feet firmly planted on worn floor planks. Meditating, I touched grounding forces deep within the planet. I was the human equivalent of Tesla's light bulb powered through its connection to the earth.

After class, the leader approached me. She asked, "What did you feel?"

"A surge of energy."

She said, "What kind of energy?"

I answered, "It was without purpose."

She asked, "What is your goal?"

I thought back to my college years. "To get past the physical, navigate the spiritual, and find meaning in my life."

She said, "I have two gifts for you." She handed me a pedometer. "This will help you plod your life's 87 million steps."

"What do you have for my spirit?"

"This message. Your heart has been allotted two-and-a-half billion beats. Use wisely the remainder."

I used the pedometer for a year or two.

***

I was fifty. I heard of a wise man, Yoshi-san. I traveled to Japan to meet this septuagenarian highly regarded by scientists and shamans alike.

We met for lunch outside on a concrete bench. He brought his 113-year-old mother's buckwheat noodles and spoke at length of their preservative powers.

I asked him, "How many steps are we given?"

He dug a pedometer from his pocket, "10,000 steps so far this day."

I asked, "How long will I live?"

He answered, "You walk in a series of diminishing halves that may never end." Then he rose, turned, and disappeared into the blossomless cherry trees of Sakurazaka Park.

Back home, I rummaged in the attic until I found my pedometer.

***

I am a centenarian in Colorado. I draw energy from granite mountains and intravenous feeding tubes. I no longer take footsteps or tally heartbeats. I lie in this bed among machines and pumps. And stare at the empty white ceiling.

I think back to my college days and Zeno's words—one-half of your travels will always remain.

***

I'm on a remote lake. Overhead, a billion stars consume the moonless sky. I find beauty in the patterns of Milky Way's gossamer lace. The Gordian knot loosens. Its strands unravel.

I fear only the collapse of Zeno's paradox...and the breaking of his promise.

Mike Summers grew up playing with lots of dangerous stuff, such as rocket fuel and dynamite. His professional life was spent primarily in Silicon Valley while also traveling the world, innovating at technology laboratories. Mike is finally getting to write about the many wonderful ideas and worlds he's seen and imagined.

Duffy's Footprints

Duffy was born on the streets of New Orleans in the wake of hurricane Katrina. When I first met him, he was a frightened ball of black fluff who'd been plucked out of chaos, endured a long scary trip in a truck filled with other rescued dogs, and handed over to a total stranger. But he was as eager to start his new life as my companion as I was to have a new buddy in my lonely life after all my kids had grown and gone.

It was winter in Maine and snow was another new experience for a Southern-bred pup, but he reveled in it, running along with his nose to the ground plowing up furrows of snow as he went, leaving puppy prints in his wake.

Then came what Mainers call mud-season: when frigid temps begin to warm and the frozen earth begins to thaw, it's all about mud. Duffy loved that too and then there were muddy little trails all over my house. Duffy loved my dad who lived next door and enjoyed visiting him in his woodworking shop, which of course, meant bringing lots of sawdust home to my carpets.

A gentle, friendly dog, Duffy loved everyone he met and pretty much everyone loved him back. You could say he left his prints on a lot of hearts and lives along the way, from the elderly gentleman who insisted on getting to his arthritic knees to play with Duff when he accompanied me to work to everyone who greeted him over the fence after we moved to Summerhaven, Florida.

Duffy was part Flat Coat Retriever and part Australian Shepherd and he wasn't quite sure if his job included retrieving things or herding my grandchildren, so he did both. At our summer place on an island in New Hampshire, he was in the water whenever anyone else was, swimming circles around our activity and snatching the frisbee whenever he could. When they weren't in the water the grandkids often pulled out the costume bin and Duffy stood patiently as they dressed him up; sometimes a bride, sometimes a fairy, or a dancer with a tutu. He was just as good-natured when waiting with gentlemanly manners for them to share whatever treat they had to eat.

Duffy was my companion, my solace, my welcome home, my buddy and my protector. He reveled in our daily walks on the beach where he frolicked in the ocean, poked his nose into every pile of seaweed, and tore around the beach in glorious freedom. His swim always ended with a roll in the sand which left him looking like a sugar donut, and playing with a ball meant digging a hole for the ball to roll into so he always came home salty and sandy and in spite of a shower, still managed to bring traces of salt and sand into the house on his furry webbed feet.

We don't have a yard so Duff and I walked several times a day, sometimes just to get the job done, but most times more leisurely. Duff, of course, had to take time to check every K-9 calling card left since his last trip out, but it was a companionable time for us whether it was a long walk in the sunshine or a quiet walk in the dark of night. I can still feel the brush of his soft fur against my bare leg in the dark and feel the tug of the leash when he wanted to take a detour or stop to check out a tortoise.

Our deck was his domain and Duff appointed himself my social director. Not only was he eager to greet everyone who walked by, but he wanted me to join him. He'd come to my desk and prod my wrist with his nose.

"C'mon, Mom. There's someone here. You need to say Hi." And he was very insistent about it, so of course, I got up and went out to say hi, whereupon, he'd lie down, his job done.

And there is nothing in the world like coming home, whether you've been gone ten minutes to the corner store or all day on errands, to a pooch who greets you at the door, tail awag, totally thrilled to see you. Duffy had one other way of greeting me, something my brother called a "doggy hug." He'd shove his whole head between my knees and wait for me to pat him, and I am so going to miss those loving, eager greetings.

Duffy never slept on my bed, but he curled up next to it where I could drop my hand down and feel his furry self any time I wanted. My entire house is filled with footprints he has left behind. Not the kind I can vacuum up or wash away, but the kind that are imprinted on my heart for the rest of my life.

When the grieving is easier, I'll welcome another dog to share my digs and my life, but he – or she – is going to have some mighty big footprints to fill. Goodbye my sweet, loving Duffy. I am so going to miss you.

Skye Taylor is a novel-writing, globe-trotting, parachuting mother and grandmother who's served as a Peace Corp and USO volunteer. She loves books, writing, beaches, and history. Her published works include Bullseye, The Candidate, The Cameron's of Tide's Way series, and Iain's Plaid. Visit her website at www.Skye-writer.com

Footprints at Shambhala

The night I first saw the footprints, it was late. After working all day and into the night, I was in no mood for a stalker. But there they were… stretching from the gravel drive, across the new concrete carport and onto the porch. I could tell that whoever left them had run across the concrete, not sauntered or skipped. They tracked oil from a nearby puddle. They also only used the balls of their feet. Did I mention I teach Forensics?

Chills ran through my body. Electric ice. My breath came quicker. I felt anger more than anything else. It had been years since I was accosted. Some jerk had decided I was his one and only and he was delusional enough to think I'd be happy about it, too. His fantasy ended when I came home and discovered he'd built a fence around my entire front yard, without asking, and planted a vegetable garden inside it. I told him to leave. In seconds, Prince Charming transformed from PC into Psycho Killer. As you might have guessed, I survived. But it was weeks before I could sing again or even speak. So I moved. I wanted to get as far away as I could… from him and from the memory of what happened that night. But these footprints brought it all back.

After that initial trauma, my plan was to find a small place in a rural community, where I could live a peaceful life, uninterrupted by other people's fantasies — a tall order for a psychologist. The irony did not go unnoticed with my friends, but I was bewitched by possibility. Moreover, I'd recently visited such a place. It was a haven of sorts for some of the most creative people I've ever met. Yes, the journey was complicated but soon I'd closed my private practice, started a new job search, pulled out my savings to live on until the latter came through, and put a deposit on a place that was dirt cheap. When asked why I was moving, my stock answer hinted about self-discovery. Now, I understood exactly what that meant.

In my new place, along with the multiple blessings of becoming a seashore mountain lady — thank you, Kate Wolf — I made some amazing friends. Living every beautiful fantasy I could imagine, I grew flowers in the field surrounding my house, put up a wooden arch with climbing vines, and painted inside and out. Soon, my dirt-cheap single-wide looked like the most adorable cottage ever. During this rare time, in moments of bliss, I never anticipated just how many people who are trying to escape the law, are also looking for such a place. The footsteps on the concrete pad of my carport were just the beginning of this realization.

After an initial jolt from the footprints, there was another clue that not all was well in Shambhala. It was a horrible smell and it seemed to come out of nowhere. It really gave me the creeps. The closest thing I could imagine that might create that stench was rotting flesh. Within hours, I had plumbers crawling all over and under, looking for the source. They found none. Whatever had been there, was no longer. But with the weather getting colder and windier, I had things to do and temporarily forgot about the prints, until I started hearing a banging sound. It was late at night that I began hearing something that sounded like a door swinging in the wind. Yet, when I checked each of the doors that provided access to my little cottage, I found no smoking gun... nor swinging door, for that matter.

It was the next day that I made a fascinating discovery. There was indeed another door. It opened to a closet-size room that housed the hot water heater. I hadn't seen it until now because it was located on the side of the cottage that backed up to the woods; a side I rarely visited. Could it be that the stalker was accessing my cottage through these woods? Knowing it would soon be nightfall, I tried to secure it. But when I was unable to do so, I still felt relatively secure in the knowledge that all doors and windows, that provided access into the house, were locked.

That's when the stalker upped the ante. As I slowly entered slumberland, I was startled out of bed by a scream, so terrifying, that it can only be described as inhuman. As fate would have it, that was also the night my adult daughter had chosen to visit. And the scream was just outside her window. Needless to say, after hearing my stories of the other tricks the stalker was playing, she became so frightened that she swore she'd never come back here again. That left me in the unenviable position of having to choose between my cozy cottage and my daughter. I knew then that I'd soon be saying goodbye to sweet Shambhala.

As if to cement the deal, the stalker played the cruelest trick of all. Somehow, he entered the hot water heater space from the outside, and made his way up, into the crawl space above my bed. All night, I heard heavy, slow movements only feet above my head. Was this what he'd been working up to? Was his plan to spy on me during the night? I refused to go outside, with this strange man present, so I covered myself with extra blankets and attempted sleep... unsuccessfully. This time, instead of counting sheep, or whatever else people do these days, I thought back to all the clues the stalker had left, beginning with the footprints.

Immediately, I knew who the stalker was. As it turns out, my stalker was a mountain lion, trying to stay warm in our extreme winter. That's when I finally relaxed. And as she disappeared into the nearby mountains, I disappeared into my writing.

Nadine Vaughan moved from her parents' home at 17, to travel. From Scotland, she travelled to Machu Picchu and trekked Amazonia. In California, she earned a PhD in Existential Psychology, worked as an clinician, a college professor, and producer of plays. In Florida, she's authored novels, children's books and writes screenplays.

The Pink Slippers

"Cathie?"

Surprised that my neighbor had hailed me by name on such a cold evening, I pivoted toward his raspy voice, then hesitated. Mindful of the thin layer of ice beneath me, I checked my footing before turning. Much to my amusement, my boots had etched a tight circle of chubby exclamation points when I reacted to his call. Giggling, I raised my head in a grin.

"Hi, Gus." Addressing him by name was odd. I knew nothing about my elderly neighbor, except that he wasn't prone to chatting, especially on dank nights. Although we had introduced ourselves when I moved in last year, we never spoke, settling instead for spartan smiles and wanton waves.

"Got a minute?"

"Sure." I obliged the old man's unusual bidding. Illuminated by a pale light, Gus appeared cheerful, though significantly older and more frail than I remembered. Picking up a plastic bag, he unfolded his rangy frame and bounced a package to his chest with a Parkinsonian tremor.

"I hope you don't mind, but I have something for you." His voice faltered, belying an otherwise perky demeanor.

"For me?" Thinking the offer more than a bit odd, I reacted with raised eyebrows and forced smile.

"Yes. These were Josie's."

Josie? Was she a wife? A daughter?

"She was the love of my life," he responded gently to my unasked question. "Died two years ago. Cancer. I could never bring myself to get rid of her things, but now it's time. I'm moving to assisted living. Goodwill came earlier today for everything else, but... I couldn't part with these." He cast his eyes downward for a few long seconds and then directed a steady gaze at me. "They're slippers. Last gift I gave her. She told me the morning she died that she'd always wanted pink slippers. Imagine that. After fifty-six years of marriage, I never knew. She wore them only once. I'd like to give them to someone special. You."

"Me?" I added to that question a chubby exclamation point.

"I'm sorry." Gus's voice now matched the tremble in his hands.

"Perhaps this is too presumptuous, but you remind me of her. When she was young." He glanced down at my feet. "She even wore high-heeled boots. She would have liked you."

Realizing how difficult this must have been for Gus, I composed myself quickly.

"I'd be honored," I managed to utter as I ascended his porch and accepted a dead woman's slippers. Creepy. "Thank you."

"No, thank you." His emphasis was warm, unlike the icy swirl of wind that gusted from the Gulf. He tugged a cap snuggly around his bald head. We bid each other a good night. How sad, I thought as I retraced my footprints home.

Dropping the package inside the door, I wiggled out of my coat and went about my evening routine. I fired up the wood stove, put on PJs, ate leftovers. Before snuggling in with a good book, I made a cup of tea and stoked the fire. In the midst of wrapping myself in an afghan, I spotted and retrieved Gus's package.

Tissue paper cradled two pink slippers. I'd never had pink slippers. I scrutinized the curious hand-me-downs. Mules, I corrected myself as I admired their backless profile.

"Thanks, Gus," I shrugged and plunged my feet into a softness that filled an emptiness in my soul, one I didn't know existed until that moment. "Thanks, Josie." With comfy feet, I burrowed into my leather sofa for a quiet evening and a good read. But I never got beyond the first few pages.

A deep sleep of flowered meadows and puffy skies overcame me. The world was new, as if I were a baby. A soft woman—perhaps a mother— enveloped me with laughter and lavender. Braids flying, I gathered flowers and jumped ropes. When I awoke at dawn, the fire had died out and my book was on the floor. I had never fallen asleep on the sofa. And awakened so refreshed. With vivid memories of sun-filled dreams, I got ready for work and didn't give my fanciful night another thought. Until I got home.

When I rounded the corner, I noticed that Gus was gone; his house was dark. I couldn't thank him for his gift, this time sincerely. A vague sense of regret dissipated as I went about my evening. Skipping the pretense of reading, I donned pajamas and Josie's mules. Fluffy and springy, they were like marshmallow clouds. I wrapped myself in the afghan and fell asleep.

Against those marshmallow clouds and with aging hands, the same soft woman braided my long hair, then twisted it through schoolgirl angst, college confidence, and budding womanhood. Then a tall man with a sparkling smile caressed my tresses, brushing them all night. Until my scalp tingled. Like the residue of spilled honey, the stimulation clung to my own short-bobbed hair all day.

I rushed home to my new routine. The man of my dreams materialized. Elegant. Extravagant. Kisses. Snowflakes. Sunny mists. Marriage gifts. Soft woman old. Soft woman gone. Child unborn. Anguish borne. Acceptance found. Silky gowns. Plumes of herons, feathers of down. Satin shoes. High-heeled boots. Passion erotic. Travels exotic. Secluded sands and seas of foam. Salty air. Cozy home. Speeding years. Fading years. Graying hair. Then no hair.

"Thanks, Gus," I said in the morning as I traded slippers for boots.

"Hi, Josie," I said in the evening, trading boots for slippers and fanciful repose.

But that night I awoke before dawn, distraught. My head ached, pain consumed my innards. Something was wrong. Very wrong. The dreams had turned. The fire had died. I got up and stirred the embers to life. I brewed tea. Nothing soothed me.

Sinking back into the sofa, my eyelids shuttered me into the nightmare of a dark room. No, I told the gentle man who no longer smiled. He cried. I cried. Not tonight, Gus. No meds tonight. No meds this morning, no meds tonight, I moaned over and over. Then the room got brighter. Pink. Slippers. Tonight, Gus. I'll take my meds tonight. All my meds. Tonight. I smiled at my pink-cloud feet. He kissed my hands. Consent. Morphine. Bliss.

I bolted awake and stared at the slippers. Intimate footprints of a woman I'd never known. Footprints that flashed before her dying eyes. Footprints that were her birthright and now my legacy.

"Josie," I whispered. "Josie, Josie, Josie." I removed the slippers and cradled them to my breasts. Yearning for my own pink slippers when my life would flash before me, I closed my eyes. Chubby footprints merged with soft pink ones. I opened my eyes and nodded.

Barefooted, I walked across the room and knelt before the fire. I opened the stove door, placed the package inside, and quickly latched it. "Rest in peace, Josie. Rest in peace, Gus." Rising, I blessed myself, something I had only seen, nothing I had ever done, wondering if I did it right. "Rest in peace, Cathie."

As I climbed into my own bed for the first time in nearly a week, I wondered if the smoke from the chimney turned white like when a pope is elected.

Patti M. Walsh has been a storyteller since her first fib. She's been published in Old Mountain Press, Success.com, and various trade publications. A member of the Pelican Pens and the Thomas Jefferson Writers' Group, she blogs at *WhatTheCatsAreReading.com* and lives in Fort Myers, Florida.

His Footprints

The sun was high above the aquamarine water, sparkling on the surface like scattered diamonds. A salty breeze kissed the coconut palm trees as they swayed and danced by the shore.

Niki watched the ocean waves make intricate lace patterns on the sand as she walked, deep in thought. She held on to her floppy straw hat as she looked up to the sun, warming her face.

What a beautiful day in a beautiful place! I love it here. It makes me feel so alive again and so very thankful.

Her slim fingers caressed the gold necklace she always wore; a gift from a very special someone. She promised herself she would never take it off.

He knows me so well. It was the absolute perfect gift to celebrate our new journey together.

She looked back down, shuffling her feet at the water's edge, watching as her bare feet made their own unique footprints in the wet sand.

Footprints can tell you so much about a person. You just have to pay attention to the message. A footprint can reveal a person's identity almost as well as a fingerprint. They are fascinating to study.

Niki noticed a set of large deep footprints, small shallow ones and even some tiny paw prints. So many different types of prints, no two alike, each with their own story.

She imagined the small prints belonging to a little girl, her father at her side. His deep prints meant he was probably a tall, muscular man. Niki imagined a little puppy running along the beach, chasing a ball, splashing in the water.

I'll bet this was a happy family enjoying a beautiful day at the beach, the sun streaming down while the little girl giggled at the antics of her puppy. Mama was probably basking in the sun as she lay on her beach towel.

As Niki continued her stroll, she saw a set of footprints surrounded by a circle of sea shells. Inside the circle were initials and a heart: AM loves CK. The idea of two young lovers holding hands and sharing kisses on the beach made her smile.

Something shiny caught her eye in another footprint further along the beach. She bent down to find a tiny charm in the shape of a dolphin. Niki looked up, but no one was around. She left the charm lay in the footprint in case someone came back to look for it.

Does this tiny charm have special meaning to the owner? Did they enjoy feeding dolphins? Had they swam with them? Played in the ocean with them? What did it symbolize? I hope they come back this way and find their lost treasure.

Niki rubbed her fingers over the gold necklace she wore. Footprints had special meaning to her now as she used her imagination to see and feel who made them in the white sugary sand. Each and every pair told a story.

I love to walk the beach and imagine who was here and what their story was. You can close your eyes and visualize those people who left their mark in the sand.

She sat on the beach for a while and tilted her head to the sun, waiting to see a very special pair of footprints in the sand. The warm breeze lulled her into a brief nap.

When she woke, she saw what she was hoping to see. The pattern of those footprints was familiar and very, very special. It showed that people could overcome pain, tragedy and obstacles. It showed his strength, courage and determination.

The pattern was that of a man's left footprint and a right flat oblong blunt print. It made her so happy to see them that she laughed with joy to see a man running down the beach in his unusual gait. He was wearing a prosthetic leg and making his own unique set of footprints.

Sam's here! I'd know his footprints anywhere. He is a strong man who is an example of how love and tenacity can overcome a tragedy.

Niki walked up the beach to meet the handsome man halfway. He bent over to catch his breath and smiled as she approached him.

Their first year of marriage had been both amazing and devastating. The accident changed their lives in ways that were hard to image. However, love got them through the difficult time and they grew even stronger.

He moved towards her and kissed her gently. His hand rested lightly on her slight baby bump, another sign of their strong bond of love. Their son bumped against Sam's hand, letting them know he was there too.

Baby is happy to see his dad too. What we have overcome has made us into a stronger unit; a real family now.

Niki looked down at their footprints in the sand.

They tell our very own unique story.

She reached up again to touch the gold necklace that Sam gave her. It said everything that needed to be said. The charm was two pairs of footprints with the inscription, 'Together we'll take one step at a time, now and forever.'

Sharon Weatherhead has been a freelance writer for many years. She and her husband are cruise addicts and love to travel. Making music and writing are her passions. She is semi-retired and assists seniors in choosing their Medicare insurance plans.

Prey Tell

I have been following a path of unusual footprints along the tide line. The ones that just came to a complete and sudden stop. Prints that are pressed deep into the clay-like hard sand as though they are carrying considerable weight. I stepped into one with my left foot. It was broader and longer than my foot. The ten front toe marks with ridges of sand between them were like mine. Still, the strange thing was it had a narrow depression extending from the heel, like an extra toe. A hole was punched in the sand, as if by a talon, much like a giant bird of prey.

I looked both ways; the beach was deserted. The morning fog had cleared, and I could see for miles in each direction, with no sign of the owner of these unique footprints. A few gulls circled overhead and seemed to be scolding me. Or was it a warning? There was the scent of decay in the air like that from rotting Sargasso seaweed, but I saw none in the area.

When I looked back over my shoulder to where I had come from, I realized that the strange gait had increased in the last fifty feet or so. The front of the prints was deeper, as though this printmaker had started sprinting. Then they stopped. There was no place to go—simply an open, deserted beach. There was no place for anyone or anything to hide. What the hell is this all about? I had no idea what was going on.

The day was warm, but I felt a chill and untied my sweatshirt from my waist and put it over my shoulders. The fog returned, rolling in off the Gulf like a rug closing off the low early morning sun.

I again turned to head back to my car, using my footprints to guide me, but they slowly filled with sand. The strange marks were not facing the way they had been but appeared to have rotated and pointed in the opposite direction. Now, I had to reorient myself, focusing on the proper path to continue forward or return to my car. I kept the slight murmur of the shallow waves in my right ear and concentrated on that as my compass point as I returned toward my car. I know that will be parallel to the beach.

Enfolded in the fog, I called out, hoping for a response from a fellow beachgoer. I wanted to tell them about the strange prints in the sand that now seemed to be facing the way they were when I first saw them. I called out again, feeling foolish, but I did not care. I shouted; still, there was no answering call. Then I realized that I had lost the surf's sound, and I was in a sensory vacuum. Now I am baffled and gripped by increasing fear.

I stopped moving and stood caught in this gray fog that is tightening its grip around me. Years ago, I wandered out onto the low tide flats at the Bay of Fundy, a place where the returning tide can outrun a horse. There, too, the fog surrounded me with astonishing speed, and I scrambled back quickly in the direction I thought was the beach. I was aided by a constant wind direction at my back and escaped without incident. A friend lived on a coastal river in England. He told me one day, twenty-four unknowing cockle gatherers had been drowned by the incoming tidal bore in front of his house. But, I live in Florida, safe from incoming twenty-foot tides of rushing water.

Now, everything keeps changing. The slight wind there shifts direction again, seemingly, with each step. Then there is hardly any wind at all. I stop, and my nerves are tingling as I strain to pick up some sensory clue that will lead me out of this nightmare. When the light breeze stops altogether, my heart stops with it. I freeze. I have no other option because I do not know what is happening, where it is coming from, or how to get out of it. The breeze abruptly starts again as if it were waiting just around the corner for me to stumble into it. Now, it is moving, circling one way then the other. Then it stays in one direction but seems to take the shape of an annulus, and I am caught inside the interior ring trapped by the concentric circles of wind.

I hear a noise, a moaning sound that is building in pitch and volume. A tornado! I am caught inside a tornado! But as quickly as it started, the wind ended, and the next sound was like something flapping, and the annulus disappeared. The winds picked up and buffeted me from all sides like some giant being was taking flight. I was spinning, trying to keep the stinging sand out of my face. I called out one more time and thought I heard something, so I yelled again, hoping for a response. I listened to a long, drawn-out human scream.

Suddenly, there was a shriek, unlike any bird sound I had ever heard. It pierced my ears and drove me to my knees. I covered my head with my hands and pressed myself deeper into the sand. Another cry, a human sound again faded as the flapping noise moved further away. Then there was silence--no sound, no movement. It seemed like a bell jar had been placed over me, and I thought of Sylvia Plath and that I might be going mad?

I sat back on the sand, closed my eyes, and breathed deeply and rhythmically. I began to calm. As I did this, I felt the wind dissipate, and the sound of the surf returned. The side of my face warmed, and I slowly opened my eyes to see that the sun had risen higher in the sky, and all the fog was gone.

I looked around, and I was still alone beside a single trail of footprints, my footprints that had extended up the beach from the parking lot. There were no other marks in the sand.

I got to my feet, brushed the grit from my clothes, checked again in all directions, and saw no one. I headed back to my car feeling as though I had lived through a nightmare. There was no explanation for what had happened and no proof.

Farther ahead of me, I saw a place where there appeared to be a scuffle or something that had roughed up that section of the beach. I picked up the pace and began running toward it. There was a patch of sand with jumbled human footprints and those of the strange creature with the rear toe. They were tangled and gouged as though there had been some conflict. Among this mess was a single large brown feather.

Ed N. White is off the Connecticut farm. His middle-grade three-book mystery series beginning with Miss Demeanor (*The Case of the Long Blonde Hair*), written under the pseudonym Celia J., is recently published by Histria Books. *The Case of the Crooked Cat* and *The Case of the Clumsy Clown* will follow.

FLORIDA YOUTH WRITER'S PROGRAM

FOOTPRINTS

FLORIDA WRITERS ASSOCIATION
YOUTH COLLECTION

VOLUME 8

Gold:
The Print

A footprint has
Many different meanings
It is all perspective
Physical, the feel and smell of fresh earth

Our imprint on our planet
The massive mark multiplied each time
We take a step and move the Earth along with us
An emotional impression left on us by someone

We all leave behind something
Whether we realize it or not
And we cannot get rid of it
No matter what lengths we go to

It will always be there
Our footprint
Following us
Like a shadow

Dancing as it follows us
It will never leave our side
We will never stop leaving
An imprint on our planet

Cameron Smith is an energetic person who likes to play soccer and compete academically in robotics. He enjoys spending time alone as well as with close friends doing fun activities like mountain biking.

Silver:
13 Playlists for My 13th Birthday

Turning 13 during the 2020 pandemic was a big letdown. 13 years old is the transition period between a child to an adult and this changeover matters to girls out there, including me. So, it was a real bummer that I couldn't celebrate being 13 with my friends and have a birthday party like usual. But my family and friends did everything in their power to make me feel special, especially my mom.

My mom began giving me early birthday gifts a week before my actual birthday. They were small items like hair ties and chocolates. Friends gave me clothing, face masks, and creams. My dad gave me a cool smartwatch. Out of all the presents, though, one gift was the most memorable and left a footprint in my life. For weeks, my mom planned a remarkable project without me knowing.

On Monday, three days before my actual birthday, my mom took me to my monthly orthodontist appointment. After the appointment ended, I walked back to my mom's van from the small parking lot. When I opened the door, I found a wrapped cardboard box in my passenger seat.

I climbed into the car and settled myself. My mom told me to open it. Inside the box was a binder that said, "Happy 13th Birthday, Vivian!" There was a letter that my mom had typed, printed, and placed in the binder. It was a very emotional, touching, and loving note that caused both my mom and me to cry. The letter explained her idea on how to make my birthday unique, by giving me something I love and could not outgrow.

At first, she wanted to create a playlist with 13 songs for me for my 13th birthday. Then she thought even bigger and decided to create 13 playlists with 13 songs in each list.

So, she was giving me a total list of 169 songs for my birthday. Crazy, right?

Well, that was a lot of songs for her to choose by herself. She decided to ask 12 other people who love me to send her their suggested song ideas.

In the letter, she wrote the 13 songs she chose for me from the "Playlist from Mom" and why she chose them. She chose:
1. Bitter Sweet Symphony by The Verve
2. Under Pressure by Queen and David Bowie
3. Don't Go Breaking My Heart by Elton John with Kiki Dee
4. Let It Be by The Beatles

5. Bruises by Train featuring Ashley Monroe
6. My Life Would Suck Without You by Kelly Clarkson
7. Flashlight by Jessie J (From "Pitch Perfect 2")
8. Mom by Meghan Trainor featuring Kelli Trainor
9. I Won't Give Up by Jason Mraz
10. Ain't No Mountain High Enough by Marvin Gaye & Tammi Terrell
11. I Lived by OneRepublic
12. Stand By You by Rachel Platten
13. Don't Stop Believin' by Journey

Besides my mom, I also received songs from seven friends, five mentors from the Pensacola Children's Chorus (an organization I'm a member of), two of my former teachers, eight of my mom's friends, all three of my grandmothers, both of my grandfathers, two of my cousins, my sweet/annoying/loving/bossy little sister, and my dad. My mom placed them all on Pandora, a streaming music service that my whole family uses and shares. When I looked at the names of people who I know and contributed to my birthday, it was as close as getting a hug from them as I had gotten since the pandemic began.

Overall, I had 14 playlists - the original 13 playlists (169 songs) and one bonus playlist from my mom and my younger sister. Together they created an additional movie playlist of songs from movies we've watched over the years.

I discovered that the average time it'd take to listen to each playlist was 48.9285714286 or 49 minutes. So, I decided to listen to one playlist every day for 13 days. (Note: it took much longer than 13 days to listen to them all.)

Music first left its footprint on me when I was four years old. At the time I requested that music be played when I took baths. I haven't stopped playing or singing music since, except I now take showers and play my own music through my cell phone.

Music has been a part of me for more than half of my life. My mom put me in piano lessons the summer after kindergarten. I took piano lessons for five years.

My family didn't notice my big love for singing, though, until after I saw the "Frozen" movie at age seven. After that, I started singing the songs from it, particularly "Let It Go," over and over. Once my mom became tired of me singing the same line repeatedly, she offered to print the lyrics so I could learn all the words to the song. She's printed me dozens of lyrics since then.

My mom and dad said that I didn't sound terrible for a seven-year-old. I had some talent between my passion and dramatic flair. I later joined the Pensacola Children's Chorus (PCC) after a school field trip in third grade to see and hear this performing group of kid singers. After the show, I immediately fell in love with the performing arts and begged my parents to let me try out. I am now in my fourth year with PCC.

After my first Christmas show with PCC in 2017, my voice was hoarse after a week of rehearsals and four shows. My parents put me in voice lessons after that. I began working with a mentor and voice coach, Mr. Dan Signor. He helped me with breathing techniques to use my voice properly so I would never be hoarse again (and I haven't been).

I took lessons with him every week for more than a year before he moved away, but Mr. Dan Signor has left a big footprint on my singing abilities. He also helped me gain confidence and enhance my expressions.

My family comments that I always have music in me, playing in my head when I don't even realize it. They say I'm constantly swaying without even realizing it... I sway when I'm eating at the table, taking a test, writing stories, singing, sitting, or listening to a song. Sometimes I may sway because I have a lack of coordination with my body. But I know my constant swaying isn't coincidental!

I sway because the music fills me with joy. It is a big part of who I am, and I do not know where I'd be without it.

Now because of these birthday playlists (and the playlists my mom and I continue to send each other), my memories, my musical footprints, will always be around to guide me and entertain me. I will continue to grow and have more birthdays, but I won't outgrow my love for music, or these playlists created especially for me. These playlists will represent important people in my life and good times, as well as the musical notes, beats, rhythms, and lyrics that I have come to know and love.

Vivian Fernandez enjoys writing both fantasy and non-fiction, influenced by books, movies, and real-life experiences. She is a member of the Pensacola Children's Chorus. Vivian has enjoyed singing and music for more than five years. She lives in Northwest Florida with her parents, younger sister, and two dogs.

Bronze:
Life is a Footprint

Life is you making a footprint on the Earth

As you take your first step, you're a new soul
Take your last step, you now know the untold
Bringing life to this world, keeping you in mind
Duplicating your footprint, a multiplicity of times

As you leave the Earth, you no longer fear it
You let the heavens take your spirit
Your body rises up and then
Your life starts the path over again

Don't let your legacy be washed away
Like footprints in the sand on a windy day
You want the words that you meant
Indelibly remembered like prints in cement

Ela Edmonds is in the Mixed Minds Writers Club at Spark Hybrid Education Center. She plays tennis and likes to ski. She has traveled around the world and speaks three languages.

Honorable Mention:
Footprints in the Mud

Footprints in the mud
In the rise of the morning sun
Each print marking a place
Washing away without a trace

The tide rolls in
And tickles my toes
I feel the cold air
As it enters my nose

The tide is low
And leaving my toes
The sun is down
And my footprints go.

Jude D. DeStefano enjoys fishing, and soccer. His favorite subjects in school are math and Social Studies. He also enjoys playing video games.

Honorable Mention:
Earth Print

The footprints
That are left
Start small
Then slowly
Start to grow
For generations

Leaving it for the next

Pollution killing off
Animals and plants
Not thinking
About the hurt we cause
This planet...
We call home

Orian Memmott attends
SPARK Hybrid Education Center.
She is a hitter for the Tidal Wave
volleyball team and enjoys
spending time with her friends,
family, and dogs.

Honorable Mention:
The Footprints You Left

The cool morning air
With wind in my hair
So peaceful and fair
Sweet summer smile on my face

Feels like you're still there
New world has begun
Your footprints still there
Never leave my heart

Your spirit with me
I feel your presence
I love you dearly
I miss you deeply

Your footprints are left
In my heart forever

Ebelle Creve-coeur is a ballerina that partakes in activities other than school and ballet such as art, karate, and piano. The poem she wrote was dedicated to her grandfather who passed away in December 2017.

Gold:
Footsteps in the Sand

My fingers trace interwoven quilt patterns
As you speak of your desired departure.

I don't know where you will run to,
Though part of me hopes it's far,
Someplace your soul can finally run free,
scream for crisp morning air with a graceful breeze,
Dance among daisies and sing among stars.

I know how often you daydream of leaving.

I remember your list of reasons piled on the desk
I kept my sewing kit, before I moved it for your ideas.

I'll miss your requests to sew a blanket, knit a sweater,
Although as you go I'll be sure to send you my work.

I can't quite grasp the concept of saying goodbye.

I'll pray the rain doesn't fall on our quiet little shack,
So I can see your footsteps in the sand outside our front door,
Long after your departure.

Samantha Leslie is a 16 year old from Lakeland, that has always possessed a passion for storytelling. She loves traveling and spending time with family, friends, and her dog, Teddy.

SILVER

Silver:
For the Tide

On a crisp day full of
Maroon sweaters and drying
Leaves, like a cracker
Under the burning wick of the sun
There is a place where the kids have stopped playing
Yet a broken heart lingers

It is tinted with echoes of another life
In another place, under another sky
Footprints of fools who have stepped in
Only to walk out
And then every living hour is in the presence
Of another

Where do all those people go
The ones who bought you flowers
Down at the store or sold you popcorn
On a rainy day or told you stories
Dozing off in the subway
Or, perhaps, stayed for longer

I wonder if we were always part of each other's history
When we danced in the ocean mist
Kicking up sand, laughing about noon
Leaving traces of our soles everywhere
And gone as fast as
The tide takes them in

Carolyn Chen is a student from Jacksonville, Florida, who has always enjoyed reading and writing. In her free time, she often draws, plays the violin, or brainstorms new ideas for stories

Bronze:
Blackmore High

Emeril stared up at the red bricked high school as the wind blew into his pitch-black hair. It was he and his older brother Cooper's first day at this new school. The school gave him an edgy feeling that he didn't like. Suddenly a swarm of people were making their way inside as Emeril stood and watched. When he realized what he was doing he immediately stopped. Help Me! Emeril jumped as he was startled by the voice. He looked all around while other students wondered what was wrong with him. The bell rang which distracted him from his thoughts. He frowned as he was going to be late on the first day.

Emeril entered the school and walked down the hallway that was starting to get empty. Half way through class, it happened again. Help Me! Emeril slammed his fist down on his desk to drown out the voice, and as he looked up everyone's eyes were on him. He expected them to laugh at him, but instead they looked dead serious. Emeril gulped and raised his hand. "May I be excused?" The teacher nodded, not saying a word and Emeril rushed out of the classroom.

As he was walking he saw something on the hallway floor. It looked like a black footprint. It was barely noticeable. He knelt down and reached out to touch it. When he pressed on the footprint, he noticed one of the locker doors flew open. Emeril's eyes widened and looked back at the footprint only to see that it was gone. He stood up and slowly approached the locker. There was nothing inside but a single white card. He took it and read what it said. "When it gets dark, come back and follow the footprints so that I can be found." The bell rang, as Emeril thought how strange it was that first period was over. The halls started to fill with students and Emeril quickly shut the locker door and hurried to his second period class.

***

When the last bell rang Emeril ran out of the school as quickly as possible. Part of him wanted to go home and forget all about the strange note, but the other part of him was curious to find out where the footprints would lead him. He decided to go wait at the cafe that was near his school. He ordered a muffin and read over the note and waited until dark.

Emeril walked back to the school and got chills. It looked even scarier in the dark. He slowly entered the building through an unlocked window of a classroom and started walking down the hallway when he heard something click from under his foot. He looked down and saw a black footprint, similar to the one he saw earlier today. When Emeril looked up, he saw his brother walking towards him. "What are you doing here?" Cooper glared at him, umm, you asked me to meet you here, there was a note at home. A note, Emeril said confusingly. Whatever, what are you doing here? Emeril huffed and showed his brother the note that was in his pocket. Cooper read it then burst out laughing. His laughter echoed throughout the halls. "You know this is a prank, right?"

Emeril snatched the card back. "Well if you think it's a prank then go home. Something's off about this school." Cooper hesitated for a second then sighed. "It wouldn't be very responsible of me to leave you here without supervision, now would it." Emeril rolled his eyes then studied the footprint. He noticed that there were actually small letters printed on it. HELP ME! Emeril winced as the voice got louder while Cooper had a surprised scared look on his face. Emeril continued to read the footprint, "Fe, Cr, O, Ag... these could be any random letters he thought. Then he remembered, "I've seen these letters on the periodic table in my Science class." Cooper raised an eyebrow. Emeril jumped up and raced down the hallway to his science class. Cooper followed him confused.

They reached the classroom. "Now what?" Cooper asked. Emeril scanned the room then spotted a plastic copy of a periodic table that was on the back wall. Right above it was a black footprint. Emeril didn't know what these footprints meant or what they represented but he was compelled to find out. He walked over and slowly pressed the footprint, expecting another clue but instead the whole wall shifted. It was like a secret passageway. Emeril grabbed his brother and pulled him through the opening. The wall closed behind them. Emeril heard the voice again. It seemed closer this time. "Help me…"

The brothers made their way down the spiral staircase that led to a small room. In the center of the room was a small frail girl who was chained. "This just got weird," Cooper whispered. Emeril slowly approached her. The voice he's been hearing was actually a real person. The girl looked up and her bright blue eyes widened so big Emeril thought she would explode. She smiled gratefully. "My angel." She then pointed to one of the walls. The two boys turned and saw a small black footprint in the middle of it. Emeril pressed it and the brick under the footprint slid out like a drawer, revealing a golden key. Emeril took it then unchained the girl. She stood up, wobbling. Her clothes were dirty and torn. "What's your name?", Cooper asked her. She steadied herself and said, "Melonie." He looked her over. "Well Melonie, we should get out of here."

***

At the police station, the officers gave Melonie some clothes and

Emeril and Cooper told the police what happened. They led the police to the school to show them the room they rescued Melonie from. However, the school was nowhere to be found, only a dirt ditch. Apparently, Blackmore High didn't exist. "This is crazy," Emeril said, wide eyed. "We went to this school for a whole day! How does it not exist!? I am NOT crazy!" One of the police officers scratched the back of his neck and glanced at Emeril worriedly. "Are you feeling ok son? Emeril just stared at the cop and his eye twitched.

"Boys!" Emeril and Cooper turned around and saw their mother running towards them. "What is going on?" she said, sternly. Cooper crossed his arms. "You tell us. You sent us to some school that doesn't even exist." "Really? because McKinley High School called me and said you both were absent for the whole day." Cooper and Emeril glanced at each other. "McKinley High School?"

Kayla Brown was born in Atlanta, Georgia and is a current resident of Pensacola, Florida. She is in the 9th grade at Booker T Washington High School. She enjoys writing fiction fantasy stories and drawing. She hopes to become a writer one day.

Thrills & Chills

Florida Writers Association Collection, Volume 14 and Florida Writers Association Youth Collection, Volume 9

The theme for our next book in FWA's Collection series is *Thrills & Chills*. Florida Writers Association Collection, Volume 14, set to be published in the fall of 2022. It will include the youth collection contest, Volume 9, with the same theme.

Our writing theme for the 2022 FWA Collection contests is "thrills & chills." This is a popular genre for writers worldwide. It doesn't take a lot of describing. It's about writing something that will thrill, jar, excite, or chill the reader. It doesn't have to be rude, crude, gory, or even heinous. There is something to be said about a story that simply evokes thrills or chills, and that works. Think of things that scare little children – practical jokes, or weird looking clowns. Write about a thrill or chill you got from something and what that something was. As always, for the Collection, fiction, nonfiction, essays, and poetry submissions are all eligible.

These short story contests, sponsored by the Board of Directors of Florida Writers Association were created to offer our members an opportunity to be published, and another way to grow their writing skills.

Each year, the contest has a new theme. All writing must conform to that theme and must be within the total word limitations as set forth in the guidelines.

The annual contests are fun—they give you the opportunity to submit two entries. They stretch you, giving you parameters and guidelines within which you previously may not have considered writing.

All judging is done on a blind basis. Submissions are posted by only title and number for the adult collection contest and by only title, number and author age for the youth collection contest. The number is assigned consecutively as stories are received. In the adult collection contest, judges read each entry entirely and evaluate according to how well it was written, was it strongly on theme, and did it strike a chord with them. Because the youth collection contest separates the entries into two age groups, judges also consider the writing-skill sets for each age group along with the same criteria as the adult contest. As with any judging, there is some subjectivity to the process. However, the judges understand that each entry selected as a winner must be ready for printing, as no editing is allowed after submission other than fixing minor typos that happen to be caught during the audit.

Next year is our sixth year for the Royal Palm Literary Award Competition Published Book of the Year winner as our Person of Renown for the collection book. This concept is inspiring our members in their writing journeys and providing yet another way for members to become published authors.

As in the past, our Person of Renown will select their Top Ten Favorite entries out of the judges' top sixty only in the adult collection contest. The youth contest winners are determined by highest scoring judges' total…and we'll be off and running with another book for the Collection, and another set of contests to look forward to for the following year.

Made in the USA
Columbia, SC
07 December 2021

50615492R00128